A SAINT IN A HURRY

A SAINT IN A HURRY

depicts the foundation of the Society of Jesus, by St. Ignatius Loyola, and the missionary career of his great disciple, St. Francis Xavier, in the Indies and Japan.

"St. Francis Xavier", says the *Catholic Encyclopedia*, "is considered the greatest missionary since the time of the Apostles. It is truly a matter of wonder that one man in the short space of ten years (6th May, 1542—2nd Dec., 1552) could have visited so many countries, traversed so many seas, preached the Gospel to so many nations, and converted so many infidels."

[*Frontispiece*

RICARDO CALVO AS ST. IGNATIUS LOYOLA
AND ALFONSO MUÑOZ AS ST. FRANCIS XAVIER

A SAINT IN A HURRY

El Divino Impaciente

THE STORY OF SAINT FRANCIS XAVIER

By
JOSÉ MARÎA PEMÁN

Translated by
HUGH DE BLACAM

With Introduction by
REV. C. C. MARTINDALE, S.J.

London
SANDS AND COMPANY
15 *King Street, Covent Garden*
W.C. 2

Nihil Obstat:

Patritius Lyons
Censor Theol: Deput:

Imprimi Potest:

✠ Josephus Cardinalis McRory
Archiepiscopus Armacanus
Totius Hiberniæ Primas

14° Feb. 1935

First published 1935

Printed in Great Britain by Sherratt & Hughes, at the
St Ann's Press, Manchester

A. M. D. G.

INTRODUCTION

The knowledge that this play was written by a Spaniard and has been performed to crowded audiences all over Spain may distract us from the play itself, so violent is the contrast between the two enthusiasms—that which is elicited by those two national glories of Spain, glories too of the world, Loyola and Xavier—and the 'enthusiasm' of the crowds that burn down Jesuit houses, wreak atrocities upon nuns and priests, and sacrileges upon the Sacred Host. This play, and the reception given to it, are therefore things to thank God for.

We can, too, be grateful for the play because it presents St. Ignatius and St. Francis Xavier so vividly to our eyes, and does so both without weakening their Spanish character—how should the author do that, being himself Spaniard of the Spaniards?—and without making it seem exotic to our Northern eyes. This is partly due to the great skill of the translator. You feel he has been faithful to his original, and yet he never makes the courtly appear pompous; the stately, grandiloquent; the ardent, fanatical; the passionate, sentimental. His choice of 'short Saxon words' might, from one point of view, seem fatal. How should these represent the sonorous Spanish? We are too ignorant to be able to tell whether a Basque, or a man from 'rough' Navarre, would speak differently from a Castilian; but after all, Ignatius had been a courtier and a poet. No: those short words transmit the rapid, crackling spirit of the two Saints, and sacrifice, I am sure, nothing in doing so. You feel you are reading Spanish; you know you are reading English; and you perceive that the translator has no need to decorate his work with 'forsooths' and what not in order to convey that you are watching men of the Renaissance, not of our day. The author and the translator between them have, then, presented to us two Saints in a reverent, realistic yet dramatic way, of whom the one has been often too romanticized, and the other presented as too chill and academic.

But we ought also to look at the play *as* a play, not as a symptom of the modern Catholic Spanish mind at large, nor as an effort in hagiography. I doubt if ever I have read anything so economically creative of 'atmosphere'. There are hardly any 'properties'. You have none of those wearisome descriptions such as you find at the beginning of Mr. Bernard Shaw's 'acts'. Neither furniture of rooms nor features of persons require to be catalogued. You just *are*, forthwith, in the College of Ste Barbe; the little Jesuit room at Rome; the palace; Malacca; off the coast of China. The play therefore is rich in suggestion, but most economic in its actual expenditure. If it were acted before curtains, you still would get the atmosphere, and you would not feel that there was any affectation of modernity or anything else, as there was when *Hamlet* was once produced in Oxford in front of dim draperies, on the grounds that these were 'mystical', whereas everyone knew that the persons responsible could not afford scenery.

This does not mean that the play is 'toned down' and neutral-tinted. On the contrary, as I said, it is full of

Spanish fire. And there are terrible lines—the more piercing because so all-but casually introduced—the traders 'who lash their dark servants . . . counting the blows on a Rosary'. And exquisite passages, like that about the scent of roses clinging to Lefèvre after he had been tending lepers; and the intimidation of Francis by his own miracles. But never once does the author rely for his effects on horrors, or portents, or prettiness.

In short, we hope that this play will often be acted in England as well as in Ireland. The Foreword points out that no large cast is needed if the players take two or even more parts, as they can quite easily do. Nor, as we said, need the scenic production give any trouble. I cannot see why even Act III Scene 2 should have been omitted: true, it contains the sailing of a ship, but there is no need for that to be seen.

However, much will be demanded of the actors! The intense affection felt by Ignatius for Francis, yet always veiled beneath his gravity: the fire that burnt hotter than ever in Francis as he grew older, yet exploded less and less in shattering eruptions: the deep cynicism of Atayde and in fact his murderous soul, which must not be allowed to interfere with his Spanish sense of dignity nor courtly demeanour. And no one of the lesser characters can be dealt with summarily—in how few lines has the tragedy of Leonor to express itself!

Here, then, is a play as stirring as any sermon, as beautiful as the best of Ghéon's and far more simple; and full of little sentences so full of mystical profundity that they flit past you and away before you have caught more than the deep blue glinting of their wings. Francis Xavier, when seemingly for ever baulked in his desire for the Indies and to break a pathway through the *Finis Terræ*, found himself reduced to lighting a little lamp, which had gone out, before Our Lady, and fell into loving ecstasy on the strength of it. This play is able to re-light many an extinguished lamp, and to set new flames shining where there had been only darkness.

C. C. MARTINDALE

FOREWORD

THIS play, by one of Spain's brilliant younger writers —poet, novelist, essayist—was produced in the Teatro Beatriz in Madrid, on September 22nd, 1933, with Alfonso Muñoz in the part of ST. FRANCIS XAVIER, and Ricardo Calvo in that of ST. IGNATIUS LOYOLA. The play was astonishingly successful. Within a few months, its 1,000th performance was celebrated, and it continued, and still continues, to draw crowded houses at long runs in different cities of the Peninsula. Soon after the first performance, the text of the play was published by the Librería de San Martín, and admirers were able to read in their homes the noble poetry which they had heard —or had not heard—on the stage. The book was longer than the acted text, since theatrical needs had caused Act III Scene I, and several discrete passages in other scenes, to be omitted from performance. Within a few weeks, the book had repeated the triumphs of the acted play. On " Book Day ", in April 1934, it was reported in most of the bookshops in Barcelona to be the work most demanded by the public. By midsummer, it had gone into ten editions.

The work, depicting the early days of the Society of Jesus and the toils of the great missionary in the days of Spain and Portugal's glory, has a peculiar appeal in Spain to-day, when the Jesuits have been suppressed by a Government which pretends to patriotism. Señor Pemán shows how much poorer the Spanish tradition must be if the works of the companions of Loyola come ungratefully to be forgotten. A Catholic revival is stirring in Spain, far and wide, and the play both assisted and reflected that spiritual movement. It could not have achieved so much, however, if it were not a work capable of success on its intrinsic merit. A merely topical piece never would have been faithful to the lofty theme, while a merely devout, but inartistic work, would have failed to draw the multitude. In brief, the author achieved a rare thing: he wrote a play which depicts the life of a Saint with close fidelity, a truly devotional play, and he did this with such artistic craft and beauty of language that the drama holds the reader or spectator not less powerfully than highly successful secular works. He gave us a model of Catholic drama; a piece to compete fearlessly with any secular rival.

The original is written in that easy verse, full of the abundant rhyme and assonance of the Castilian tongue, which cannot be imitated successfully in English. The language, throughout almost every speech, is extremely simple, as language that soars high must be; and so most of this translation will be found in small, Saxon words. There are hardly any allusions obscure even to the ignorant, and, despite the historic and linguistic gulf, the translator has found it needful to simplify only a few sentences. (A few passages have been abridged slightly for other reasons.) In the scenes in Paris and Rome, the students and priests represent men of the most highly cultivated class of Spain's great age, and their diction has some flights of art which must be delivered with a scholarly air, preferably by speakers whose voices have the typical Jesuit restraint; but the rest of the play, in which Xavier is wrestling with the spiritual elements, and talking with men of diverse race, creed and character, is to be spoken as simply as an *Ave Maria.*

This elemental plainness, as of the Scriptures, is the stylistic merit of the play. What shall be said of the author's choice and arrangement of scenes, incidents and utterances? He has followed the authentic lives of the first Jesuits faithfully; the grand sayings of his characters are sayings that are on record from of old. To material that the Saints themselves, as we may say, thus provided, he has brought a rare artistic taste. It needed, surely, a lofty sensitiveness to bring out so justly the meaning of the words and deeds of the great. Let one example suffice. In the scene in Rome, we are wrought up with the passionate eagerness of Xavier to do great things in the world of action. After the disappointment that he endures so humbly, having conquered himself at last, so that he is willing to fill a little lamp instead of to evangelize a new world, there comes the glorious news that he has been chosen for the Mission, after all. We behold, through his eyes, the vast scope of endeavour that is before him; and it is this very moment that Ignatius chooses to counsel Francis on the interior life. Here, by a dramatic juxtaposition, the author startles us to an understanding of the true Jesuit spirit; his art gives fresh intensity to words that we might read elsewhere and forget. "In the midst of outer works, think chiefly of the inner things; it is the heart of the rose that holds together the petals."

Aoḋ de Blácam

DRAMATIS PERSONAE*
(in order of appearance)

Peter Lefèvre
Juan de Oliva
Juan de Brito
Francis Xavier
Alvaro de Atayde
Violette
Ignatius de Loyola

. . .

Father Pascal Broët
Father Alonso Salmerón
Father Diego Lainéz
Lay Brother
Don Pedro Mascareñas, Portuguese Ambassador

. . .

Don Martín Alonso de Sousa
Count de Castañeda
A Lady
A Page
Father Simón Rodríguez
Doña Leonor de Ariza
King of Portugal
First Lady
Second Lady

. . .

Father Cosme de Torres
Mansilla, a Lay Brother
Indian Children
Matthew, an Indian convert
Patamar
Indian Mother
Indian Men and Women

. . .

* In the original performance, most of the actors played two parts, and the company numbered twenty-eight persons; by further multiplication of parts played by actors, a smaller company can be made to suffice.

First Indian
Second Indian
Chief

Brahman
Chamberlain

. . .

Don Duarte de Gama,
Portuguese captain
Juan Fernández

Yagiro (Paul of the Holy Faith)
Vicar-General of Malacca

. . .

Japanese Warriors

. . .

Don Miguel de Jaso,
brother of Francis
Another Brother

Sister
A Beggar

The illustrations are from photographs of the first production in Madrid.

PROLOGUE

A parlour in Ste Barbe's College, Paris.

Around a pedestal globe stand PETER LEFÊVRE, JUAN DE OLIVA. JUAN DE BRITO, *in students' garb. On one side there is a table with papers and rolled maps. Some distance from the group, absorbed in a book, is* FRANCIS XAVIER, *also dressed as a student. Doors at either side ; a small, curtained door at the back.*

LEFÊVRE:

[*Pointing to the globe*] Well, then, and what is this that you have marked with red ink?

OLIVA:

That is the seaport of Palos, and here, just beside it, is the estuary of the river Moguer which in olden time, on account of its strange hue, was thought to flow from the depths of the underworld—from hell itself.

LEFÈVRE:

And it was from this estuary, you say, that the Genovese ships set sail?

OLIVA:

Aye.

LEFÊVRE:

And these three little ships, these caravels, they were named?——

OLIVA:

Pinta, Niña and—the largest and strongest—*Santa Maria.*

BRITO:

What lovely names!—and so simple, as if they were just for three little girls!

LEFÈVRE:

Even so. All the great works of Providence begin with things that seem petty and childish. The heron is born of an egg, and great trees of acorns. Redemption and eternal life come from an inn and from a manger. Is it so strange, then, Juan de Brito, that this great affair of the opening up of the Indies should begin—as if in contrast to its grandeur—with three small ships that bear the names of little maidens?

OLIVA:

What times these are of unheard-of marvels!

BRITO:

And how God has blessed us, Juan de Oliva, that He brought us into the world when the world is so full of wonder!

LEFÈVRE:

[*Unrolling one of the maps on the table*] See these old maps, made before our time, how they have in large letters, beyond the outline of Europe, *Mare Tenebrosum, Finis Terræ!*—the Shadowy Waters, the End of the World! Ha! what were these strange words for but to conceal the ignorance of the learned in this world's science? With terrifying names they cloaked over the littleness of what they really knew.

BRITO:

[*Pointing to the globe*] And look you, Peter Lefèvre, how they painted serpents and dragons in the unexplored places, as if to say: to go beyond this line where the world ends would be temerarious; there's nothing out there but chaos!

OLIVA:

But Spain, our Spain, dispersed that chaos—broke through that boundary line—spread over those dark, fantastic seas the light of three white sails!

BRITO:

[*At the globe*] And Portugal, Peter Lefèvre, Portugal did no smaller deed. This line shews the course of the three ships of the other squadron, Da Gama's ships, *San Rafael, Berrio, San Gabriel.* In ten days' sailing they arrived at the Fortunate Isles, and soon afterwards they turned the southernmost point of Africa, where the earth ends—they have named it the Cape of Good Hope: God grant that it be rightly named!

LEFÈVRE:

And they arrived?——

BRITO:

Even at the Kingdom of Malabar in the Indies: and the Zamorin, the emperor of that region, pledged his friendship with a thousand gifts, and sealed his promises with acts. Laden with new and goodly things, with silks of the East and fragrant gums—even as the Kings of the Orient long ago with incense and with myrrh—the galleons returned home even in less time than they had taken on the outward voyage. Their names were angels' names; and truly they winged their way with speed that did honour to those names.

OLIVA:

Almost I can imagine it all as if I were myself embarked upon the vessels. . . . Ah, but the mind reels before the enormous distances. To my mind, the planets themselves seem no farther away from us than those Indies.

XAVIER:

[*Who has raised his eyes from his book and has grown interested, little by little, in the talk*] And for my part, it surprises me to see you all so much overcome by so little.

OLIVA:

[*Mocking*] Gentlemen: our scholar has waked up!

BRITO:

[*To* XAVIER] Do you really mean to say that all these great wonders do not amaze you——

XAVIER:

No, they do not amaze me . . . but perhaps . . . I am a little jealous that it was not I myself who was the first to reach the Indies.

BRITO:

[*Mocking*] Oho, my nightingale, you are not afraid to sing!

OLIVA:

[*Also mocking*] Very holy men, I suppose, wonder at nothing?

XAVIER:

[*Half irritated, half ironical*] God knows, I wonder enough . . . but not in that fashion.

LEFÈVRE:

How then?

XAVIER:

Have you not seen simple folk in a village marvelling at the sight of some caparisoned mule? It is the novelty of the sight—a mule in fine harness—that sets them wondering; but some grand gentleman whose lackey follows him all day on a mule caparisoned in satin sees nothing strange. Habit makes all marvels common. I am not overcome by these things of which we speak, because I am dreaming of higher things. The great stone cliff does not wonder at the pebble. With you, now, it is this way: that you have so small a soul that you are like those villagers, marvelling at the world's immensity!

OLIVA:

What then? Is the whole world too small for the flight of your imagination?

XAVIER:

Maybe, even so!

BRITO:

I have it! Your Excellency designs the conquest of a star!

XAVIER:

[*Seriously*] No, not that. . . . But it seems to me that we ought to take this new illumination of the world, not as something to overpower us, but just as a new illumination of the mind. A new world has risen in our sight. Yet this is no miracle. It is but a conquest of the unknown made by the reason—the reason, clear and serene, through which this world of ours is cleared of doubt and mystery. Castile and Portugal have taught the world its limits.

OLIVA:

Most of all, Castile!

BRITO:

Portugal, most of all!

XAVIER:

Your dispute is folly! This marvel of discovery is great enough to yield equal glory to one and to the other, brothers both. [*Pointing to the globe*] See you, these two routes across the world, clear, precise, unmistakable —one towards the shadowy West, and one towards the far-off East where the twilight's born. They are the two arms of Spain, outstretched: the arms of Spain crucified. I say, of Spain, not of Castile and Portugal; for though we think that two lands have made these discoveries, in truth it is but one internal voice that has moved them with a single ideal, the voice that cries to one God, the same; aye, signed with the same symbol of the Cross they have gone their ways, Portugal to the East, Castile to the West.

[ALVARO DE ATAYDE, *also a student, has entered at the left, and looks on the group discoursing at the globe.*]

ATAYDE:

[*In a mocking tone*] So this is what the poet calls our restless youth—the springtime of life! It is Carnival time, and here are you conferring over the very planet like so many doctors in consultation over a corpse.

XAVIER:

Atayde!

ATAYDE:

How can you all endure to coop yourselves in this cage when Paris all around you is ablaze with jubilation? The streets are crammed with people; the lovely ladies of all France are to be seen, thick as flying spray upon the waterfall. . . .

OLIVA:

Atayde is right.

ATAYDE:

Come, come! Away with us to Panadero's tavern: we'll dance the galiard and the sink-a-pace!

BRITO:

[*Seizing his hat*] Nobody will say no to that.

ATAYDE:

[*Waving to all to go out*] Right, right! So—one, two, three! [*Approaching* XAVIER] Or is it that we have one dull fellow among us who would rather stay here translating Lucretius or construing Cornelius Nepos?

XAVIER:

[*Coldly*] No: it is just that there are some who see no charm in these silly masquerades, where the flush upon the face is painted, and the smiles are false and forced.

ATAYDE:

Enough of sermons! [*He takes a chair to the centre, stands on it and declaims in mock solemnity*] Gentlemen: I announce the great novelty of the day. Xavier is going to keep us company: he is coming with us to the dance.

[*Hands clapped in approval.*]

BRITO:

Right, right! Leave melancholy aside for just to-day, comrade!

OLIVA:

Bring his cloak and hat!

XAVIER:

[*Imperative*] Bring nothing!

BRITO:

What! Will you not come to-day, either?

XAVIER:

I will not come!

BRITO:

And pray why not?

XAVIER:

Because I so wish. If I had any notion of going to the dance, it is enough for Atayde to speak in that fashion to decide me to remain in the College and to go no farther. You will not change my decision. I will not go because I am resolved to set no foot within the tavern.

OLIVA:

It is all a matter of taste.

XAVIER:

A matter of birth and of breeding!

ATAYDE:

Still sermonising! You, with your put-on solemnity, are always finding fault with your neighbours.

OLIVA:

[*Mocking*] You are like the man with the sword who was afraid to draw it lest he wound himself.

ATAYDE:

Perhaps you are afraid of the big, bad world and the ladies?

XAVIER:

[*Stung*] I can carry myself as a gentleman of fashion with a feather in my hat and a swagger; but I can bear myself, too, with gravity, like my castle of Xavier among the highlands of Navarre. [*Signing towards the door at right.*] And now, let me pass.

OLIVA:

Where are you going?

XAVIER:

To bear out my words with deeds. You, go you to your dance. For me, I will go back to my Humanities. [*He goes out, firmly.*]

ATAYDE:

Every day that wet blanket annoys me more.

BRITO:

When virtue is not modest, it is mere bombast.

LEFÈVRE:

He is good . . .

ATAYDE:

He goes too far; he is cocksure of himself; he sins by extremes. He carries his merits like a new buckle on the belt—too conspicuous for good taste.

BRITO:

He is all taken up with that Spaniard who has come here to study theology.

OLIVA:

Whom do you mean? A poor, threadbare fellow, wrapped up in devotion?

BRITO:

The very man. You see that stranger with our friend always, talking earnestly, sometimes pleading. . . .

ATAYDE:

What is this stranger's name?

LEFÈVRE:

Ignatius of Loyola.

ATAYDE:

And . . . What sort is he?

LEFÈVRE:

A man much worn; nothing remarkable in person or in stature; of colour swarthy-brown, with a spare, clipped beard; but his eyes are like coals of fire, they seem to see more than they do see, they penetrate you. As for his bearing and rank, though he goes almost ragged, he has an air that tells you that he has been a gallant among the gallants, high-bred and proud. At the siege of Pamplona, where he went soldiering, he was wounded in the leg by a shot; the bones were shattered, yet by a miracle he was not disabled—he bears the trace in a limp which gives him a delicate way of walking. That is the man; but mark you, he is of the sort that goes farther than all the others. When he lay wounded in Loyola, he read the *Flos Sanctorum,* "The Flower of Sanctity", and his good Spanish blood was so stirred up by what he read that nothing will do him but to go farther than he who goes farthest—he wants to be more saintly than all the saints of other days, put together. [*Speaking in a lower tone, confidentially*] As I hear, he is about to leave for Rome with the secret purpose to obtain authority to found an Order; he has set before him some great undertaking—who knows what?—and he will succeed in it, he will triumph. Step by step, through good and ill, gentle and firm, now pleading, now commanding, on he goes—limping, limping, certain to attain his end.

BRITO:

Do you know what I am thinking, Lefèvre, when I hear you speak of him? By your manner, I think that he has captured you, like our friend from Navarre.

LEFÈVRE:

I have but described him as he is, Brito.

ATAYDE:

[*Who has been thinking for some moments*] Listen, all! I have thought of a great jest that will shake up our Xavier and this saint from Loyola.

BRITO:

Tell us, tell us!

ATAYDE:

Ha, ha—you'll see that it is rich! You know Violette—the liveliest girl in Paris. She is waiting for me, to go with us to the tavern, to the dance.

OLIVA:

Always Atayde the ladies' man!

ATAYDE:

We'll bring her up quietly to this hall and seat her in this corner, in my cloak and cap, so that she will look like another student. Then we'll strike the bell three times: that's the signal when any one is asking for Xavier in the hall. We, meanwhile, will hide behind these curtains; and won't we laugh at our hero from Navarre, when he kisses the hands of the gentleman who has called to see him, and finds that he's a girl!

BRITO:

Rich, rich!

OLIVA:

We'll catch him with bird-lime.

ATAYDE:

I will bring the lady in a trice.

[*He goes out, by the left.*]

LEFÈVRE:

These practical jokes do not amuse me. I'll have no part in this unmannerly trick.

OLIVA:

I tell you, this limping saint from Loyola is taking all of us in his nets. He'll make goody-goodies of us all. In a little while we'll have the whole College turned into a convent.

LEFÊVRE:

Hardly that! But I have no humour for jokes to-day. I am going in.

BRITO:

But promise us this: that you will not warn Xavier of the jest.

LEFÈVRE:

I am going in, to walk in the garden. I am not likely to talk to anybody.

BRITO:

That's enough.

LEFÈVRE:

So—have your sport, and may no harm come of it!

[*He goes out.* BRITO *and* OLIVA *prepare the scene.*]

BRITO:

And now, let us set the stage.

OLIVA:

Aye, quickly. Here, in this corner, put the seat.

BRITO:

[*Carrying it to the extreme left*] Farther from the curtains. If we are heard laughing too soon, it will be all up with the game.

[ATAYDE *enters, leading* VIOLETTE *by the hand.*]

ATAYDE:

Here, friends, is Violette—the loveliest lady in Paris, and the most discreet.

[*Bows, and burlesque reverence.*]

OLIVA:

Surely, there is no lady more beautiful, more stately.

ATAYDE:

For such a court-of-honour, she is just the Queen we need.

OLIVA:

The Queen of Love!

VIOLETTE:

Of Pleasure: that is the better realm to rule over!

BRITO:

Pleasure and Love—sure, they always go together.

VIOLETTE:

That's enough, boys, of pretty speeches. Where is the disguise?

ATAYDE:

It's simple enough; just my cloak and my bonnet.

[*She dons them.*]

OLIVA:

Perfect!

BRITO:

The best actor could not play the part better.

ATAYDE:

And now the seat.

[*He seats her so that her shoulder is turned towards the door by which* XAVIER *will enter; only cloak and cap will be seen, so that she will seem a student.*]

BRITO:

Shut mouths, all!

VIOLETTE:

Oh, hurry with it; for I'll burst out laughing if you're slow.

ATAYDE:

Three strokes of the bell!

OLIVA:

[*Going to a nook, where a gong stands*] Now for them. Gentlemen: one . . . two . . . three!

ATAYDE:

The curtain rises for the comedy of the Gallant Gentleman and the Pretty Lady.

[*They hide behind the curtains, and peep out.* VIOLETTE *struggles to contain her laughter. Pause.* XAVIER *enters by the right, looks around him, approaches* VIOLETTE.]

XAVIER:

Who calls me? [*Pause*] No answer?

[*He approaches the seat, impatient.*]

Is our new comrade dumb? He must uncover whether he likes it or not.

[*From behind the seat, he removes the bonnet with a quick gesture.* VIOLETTE *rises, they face each other.*]

What kind of joke is this?

[*Explosion of laughter behind the curtain; all come out.*]

ATAYDE:

Oh, here's a miraculous transformation; a man has turned into a woman!

XAVIER:

Aye, and reeds have turned into lances, Atayde! What is the meaning of this? Is it fight you're seeking? Perhaps you think that I am scared of women? This is a dull, cheap piece of humour—a joke worn threadbare, worthy of a fool's invention. Well might I guess that it was Atayde who planned it! A joke, to be a good joke, must be a joke in good taste.

[*The others are disturbed by* XAVIER'S *tone.*]

BRITO:

Sure, the thing's not worth so much fuss.

XAVIER:

You're right. I have given too much importance to such a miserable triviality. God keep you! [*To* VIOLETTE, *with ironical courtesy*] Your humble servant, my lady, is honoured, and kisses your feet (as we say): he's only sorry for the informality of your reception . . . and for such company!

[*He makes to leave, by the right.*]

ATAYDE:

Halt! To whom do you refer, Xavier, with that word?

XAVIER:

Is it not plain enough that I mean you—you follower of women of this kind?

ATAYDE:

You have always a proud answer. Answer me in another fashion!

XAVIER:

And in another fashion ask me your questions!

ATAYDE:

[*Raising clenched fists*] Like this?

[OLIVA *and* BRITO *come between them.*]

XAVIER:

[*Hardly restraining his wrath*] I will make clear to you, as you wish to know, who is this "poor Xavier", whom you think to be scared of women. [*To the others*] You others, leave this place while I deal with my own affairs. You, Atayde, wait here, till I find out whether you are scared—of a man!

ATAYDE:

As you wish. I only ask you to wait until I have con-

PROLOGUE: AT THE COLLEGE OF ST. BARBE, PARIS [p. 33

ST. IGNATIUS: . . . Men who are born, men who must die,
all of them. . .

ducted the lady to Panadero's; then, I am at your service.

XAVIER:

Then be swift. Your outrage burns my soul like a flame; I can hardly wait to teach you the quality of the men of my race and breed.

[*During these last words,* IGNATIUS LOYOLA *has entered at the right. He leans on a walking stick.*]

IGNATIUS:

Men who are born, men who must die, all of them . . .

XAVIER:

[*Surprised*] You, too?

IGNATIUS:

. . . Must die, all of them; and if their petty vanity is hurt, they bear themselves like animals.

XAVIER:

[*Seeking to excuse himself*] It was not I who caused the quarrel. It was Atayde who began it.

IGNATIUS:

And it was Christ who taught us to turn the other cheek.

ATAYDE:

It was he who cast the first insult.

XAVIER:

He invited me to the tavern, and I declined to go.

IGNATIUS:

I am not rebuking your refusal, but the manner and the form of it. You could have shown your resolve with the same firmness . . . but with greater charity.

VIOLETTE:

O, la! but all these sermons weary me. Shall we go?

ATAYDE:

[*To* XAVIER] I am going to the tavern: but I'll be back right soon. [*To* BRITO] Will you come?

[BRITO, OLIVA *and* VIOLETTE *follow him out. Before going, he mocks* XAVIER.]

And I am sorry to see, Xavier, that you are not quite the saint after all!

[XAVIER *and* IGNATIUS *remain face to face.*]

XAVIER:

You have insulted me—insulted me gravely—I will not forgive you.

IGNATIUS:

This insult, Xavier, I do not ask you to forgive; I do not ask your pardon.

XAVIER:

Your rebuke was harsh.

IGNATIUS:

Not harsher than the polishing cloth with which a cup is made to shine. The cloth does not ask the cup's pardon for making it shine more brightly!

XAVIER:

Who appointed you to be my guardian?

IGNATIUS:

Why, just compassion for your ardent spirit, Xavier. It grieves me to see your soul burning so, and yet giving neither light nor heat. You are like a rushing torrent that plunges into a desert of stones and is lost; and look you, while the river is roaring, the garden is parched for water.

XAVIER:

He does not live vainly, Ignatius, who seeks to win fame.

IGNATIUS:

A deep and deceptive pit in your path! What would it serve you to win all the world and lose your very self?

XAVIER:

Do you seek to rid me of ardour—of zeal—of ambition? —to make me give up my desire to excel?

IGNATIUS:

I do not seek to rid you of ardour. I seek to kindle it in you even more. I do not seek with a soft music to woo you into pleasant and easy ways; no, but I will put a great unrest between your soul and life; I will make you discontented as never before. I will widen you, Xavier! I will plant new thorns, new flowers, in the soil of you! I will temper you with new ardours, and I will have your life so polished with sorrow that it will be purged wholly clean of fault and error, like a lantern which is so pure that you cannot tell where the crystal parts the air.

XAVIER:

[*Pensive, after a pause; disquieted by* IGNATIUS' *words*] You ask me, then, to separate myself from all? You ask me, perhaps, to give up my fortune and my rank? You ask too much of me.

IGNATIUS:

And I offer you much more. You, the deluded seeker after fame, glory, honour, do you make little of it when

I offer you a greater fame, a finer glory? [*Pleading*] Oh, do not seek for fame and honour in shields and blazonry, in crowns and coronets. These are not what your ambition really craves; it is not to these that I summon you. You think, when applause is loud around you, that you have reached your highest destiny. Do you not see, do you not know, that your destiny is divine, and that you are resting before half your journey's done? Am I right?

XAVIER:

[*Exalted by degrees*] Perhaps, perhaps! Even as I win success on success, and grow more occupied with the world, there is something within me that seeks peace in the world and never finds it there. Aye, though I like not to confess it even to myself, I return from every quest with disappointed hopes—with lowered banner and with battered helm. [*Confidential, suppliant; seizing* IGNATIUS *by the arms*] Oh, leave me not, Ignatius, to my interior doubts! Tell me, what are these desires that never are satisfied? What is this within me that never is content?

IGNATIUS:

That which never is satisfied is the part of your being which alone remains above water when you are caught in the fatal stream; it is of that that I would lay hold to save you, even when you are drowning.

XAVIER:

Am I in such peril, do you think? Do my ambitions lie so far astray?

IGNATIUS:

It is risky walking, foot behind foot, on the verge of a

volcano's crater. Give up, I say, your idle quests, your searchings hither and thither; they lead you farther astray from your true destiny and waste your powers. Why haggle with Him who is generosity itself, why grudge Him anything?

XAVIER:

[*Hastily; he is overcome by* IGNATIUS' *earnest pleading*] Ignatius, how your words enflame my faith! But I am weak. Doubt comes again a thousand times, and a thousand times I bid myself be guided by your kind voice: but you will not believe, however often I tell you. O, you from whom I fled, lay on me your obedience; oblige me to follow you; command me, as a child is commanded although it does not wish to eat.

IGNATIUS:

Very little will I have to do, if only your will is surrendered and rightly bent. The good, grassy earth, when it wishes to bear fruit, needs no cultivator. On both sides, Xavier, the agreement is made. [*Some steps towards the door at the right*] And now, God be with you. I am going down to the garden where I left Lefèvre, to take from him some papers. . . . [*He draws near to* XAVIER, *and lays a hand on his shoulder*] Agreed?

XAVIER:

Agreed.

IGNATIUS:

And you will not go back along the path that you have left?

XAVIER:

God forbid!

IGNATIUS:

The world goes swiftly by, and behind are death, judgment, hell or heaven. To remember that is to keep your feet from the precipice. [*With affectionate irony*] And now, good novice of mine, is there anything else you desire?

XAVIER:

Nothing, Ignatius.

IGNATIUS:

God be with you, Xavier.

[*He goes out.*]

XAVIER:

[*Throwing himself on the seat*] Heaven . . . hell . . . death . . . judgment. . . .

[ATAYDE *has entered by the left in time to hear these words. He approaches, with mockery.*]

ATAYDE:

Where are the Faithful to whom your Excellency is preaching?

XAVIER:

Come, Atayde, come hither.

ATAYDE:

[*Drily*] What do you want with me?

XAVIER:

[*A slight gesture of anger. He represses himself*] I wish to beg your pardon.

ATAYDE:

My pardon?

XAVIER:

Yes: I crave pardon for the excessive words that I used; for my arrogant sayings and my foolish insults. Atayde, for all these, I humbly beg your forgiveness.

ATAYDE:

[*Suspiciously*] What new tack are you on now? What happened in my absence? Were you drinking?

XAVIER:

Oh, insult me as you will; I have deserved it. [*He flings himself on his knees at* ATAYDE'S *feet*] I, who have boasted myself to be above all others, and have sought to rule the wills of my neighbours, I have failed to conquer my own meanness, and to master my own passions. [*Exalted: bowing his face to the floor*] I am light and the clay of the field, I am dust and I am spirit, pitted against one another in perpetual strife; I am a morsel of earth that aspires to heaven; as the earth draws me down, heaven would draw me up; and there is none so vain, so foolish as I, who, dreaming of so much, achieve so little. Despise me!

ATAYDE:

Is it so that you seek to slip out of the consequences of your challenge? [*He shrugs, contemptuously*] Well, pardoned! On children and on women, a man does not draw the sword.

XAVIER:

[*An angry motion; about to rise*] Atayde!

ATAYDE:

You coward!

XAVIER:

[*Repressing himself, and bowing his face again*] Say what you will!

ATAYDE:

Idiot!

XAVIER:

Even so! Go on, go on! How sweet, and delightful like fresh water, are your insults to me!

[IGNATIUS *has come in by the right with* PETER LEFÈVRE. *They stand, viewing the scene.*]

IGNATIUS:

What is happening?

ATAYDE:

Oh, nothing. This fool—I came back to speak with him, I provoked him, and he has turned suddenly so humble that he submits to me!

IGNATIUS:

[*To* XAVIER, *severely*] And this, too, is not what I told you.

ATAYDE:

[*With a gesture of disdain*] That's all. Now, who's for the dance with me? I promise him welcome.

IGNATIUS:

[*Dismissing him with a civil gesture*] God keep you: and may He not hold you accountable for all this folly. [ATAYDE *goes out by the left. A pause.* IGNATIUS *addresses* XAVIER] You have done ill.

XAVIER:

Was it a fault to humiliate myself?

IGNATIUS:

I do not deny your generosity, your zeal; but I beg you . . . a little less of this rushing to extremes. Do not make much of your nothingness! See you, between truth and falsehood, there is only the dot of an i. To overdo humility argues a lack of humility; it is vanity itself. I would have you to be humble, but not with so much crying out about it. I would have you to serve God . . . but do not be fancying yourself as a saint!

XAVIER:

[*Sadly*] O, my Ignatius!—and I thought that I was faithful to your command.

IGNATIUS:

Be so, but not with so much unction. When the river makes a great noise, it is because it is shallow and there are stones in it.

XAVIER:

I know that you are right.

IGNATIUS:

Health is not aware of itself. It recreates its strength, without knowing it, in silence. Virtue that goes forth with great display is hardly virtue.

XAVIER:

Oh, teach me to know what is the true virtue!

IGNATIUS:

Xavier, there is no more notable virtue than to do, in all simplicity, just that which is given us to do. When our intention is simple, nothing perplexes us. The magic of the roses is just this: that, being so beautiful, yet they know nothing of it.

[*A bell sounds.*]

XAVIER:

The signal for recreation. . . . I meant to spend the time in study, but I have changed my mind.

IGNATIUS:

What, then, do you purpose?

XAVIER:

To go down into the garden. There, beside the fountain, I will take my pleasure; I will delight in the sweet dew of the evening. . . . Is that the way, Ignatius?

IGNATIUS:

That is the way, Francis. Always natural and simple!

[XAVIER *goes out at the right.*]

LEFÊVRE:

[*Who had been present all this while, a little to the rear*] How well you overcame him!

IGNATIUS:

Peter Lefèvre: I build my happiness and my hopes on Xavier. If I win Xavier, Xavier will win for me a world.

LEFÊVRE:

Do you hope for so much from his gifts?

IGNATIUS:

Yes, and from his so-impulsive soul, if only it be harnessed by meekness and good patience. When his inexperience is corrected, his vanity subdued, if he keeps faith with me, I hope for miracles of sanctity from him. . . . [*He makes to go out, but turns to* LEFÈVRE *to warn him*] But you, for charity's sake, tell him never a word of this!

[CURTAIN]

ACT I

Rome. A modest chamber in the first house of the Society of Jesus; doors at the sides, a window at the back. FATHER DIEGO LAÍNEZ, *reading;* FATHER PASCAL BROËT *and* FATHER ALONSO SALMERÓN, *conversing.*

[*As the curtain rises,* FATHER PETER LEFÈVRE *enters at the left.*]

FATHER BROËT:

Peter Lefèvre, how go those busy feet?

FATHER LEFÈVRE:

Much better than that which they carry deserves, thanks be to God.

FATHER BROËT:

You were at the hospital?

FATHER LEFÈVRE:

I was.

FATHER BROËT:

Was there much doing?

FATHER LEFÈVRE:

There was corn for the sickle and a sickle for the reaper.

FATHER SALMERÓN:

Rest yourself now. In a little while the bell will ring for the collation. [*He goes to help him to doff his mantle: he pauses an instant*] Were you in the gardens before you came up here?

FATHER LEFÈVRE:

I? No. Why do you ask?

FATHER SALMERÓN:

Because an odour as of roses in flower seems to be carried by your Reverence's soutane.

FATHER LEFÈVRE:

Ha! Don't be talking such nonsense. I to carry the odour of roses who come from tending lepers! [*He starts. He is about to say something, but checks himself*] Still . . . no, no, no; it could not be.

FATHER BROËT:

What were you saying?

FATHER LEFÈVRE:

Nothing—nothing of consequence.

FATHER LAÍNEZ:

[*Who has listened silently, laying down his book*] Father Lefèvre I put you under obedience. Say what you were going to say.

FATHER LEFÈVRE:

Why, then—and what I say, may it redound to the greater glory of God!—this evening I had to hear the dying confession of a leper, one who in days past was a notorious evil-liver. It cost me hours of strife to bring his soul to contrition—to win from the dross of his evil state that little vein of gold which the Lord has denied to none; with patient toil, at last I dug through to the ore. When he was absolved from his sin, a great consolation overwhelmed the poor fellow. He embraced me with such fervour that his sores rubbed my soutane; perhaps these were the roses that yielded such a scent!

FATHER SALMERÓN:

Ah, there! Don't you smell it?—don't you smell it? The scent of roses has filled the whole house!

FATHER LAÍNEZ:

[*Severely*] What a strong imagination you have, Father Salmerón! If Father Ignatius heard you, he would call you a day-dreamer. [*To* FATHER SALMERÓN] Open the window, Father. [*He beckons them to him and points*] See! the gardens in flower. March is passing, and April's on the threshold: springtime in Rome, that was all that you smelt. [*All gaze out*] Why look for miracles and marvels, without need? Look you! Springtime! What greater miracle could you conceive?

[FATHER IGNATIUS LOYOLA *enters at the left in time to see them gazing ecstatic from the window; he approaches.*]

FATHER IGNATIUS:

What is the wonder?

FATHER SALMERÓN:

The colours of this garden, which fills all the neighbourhood with pleasant scent.

FATHER IGNATIUS:

[*He too looks forth for a moment.*]

Yes, it is lovely. Now close the window. Flowers weaken the will.

FATHER BROËT:

Were you at the Holy Father's Curia?

FATHER IGNATIUS:

I was there, making petition concerning some papers that are overdue, papers necessary for the expedition to the Indies, and the Mission.

FATHER SALMERÓN:

Portugal, as I understand, desires six missionaries for the East?

FATHER IGNATIUS:

Aye, and how well pleased I would be to give them if the Society had them! This time, the expedition must be satisfied with two or maybe three. Look you, there are ten of us, workers in the vineyard, and the vineyard is the whole wide world! It cost me no small sorrow to have to say this to the ambassador, Mascareñas.

FATHER SALMERÓN:

May the Lord guide you to a fit choice of men for the work: that is what matters. Let them be good servants of God, though there be no more than a couple of them, and, sooner or later, they'll gather a goodly harvest.

FATHER IGNATIUS:

You speak with truth's own voice, my son. Give me workers few but good! The Lord is content with these, and thereby shows the more clearly that it is He who does the work. As for this sowing of the seed in the East, I purpose to give the task to Father Simón Rodríguez, and to Bobadilla.

FATHER LAÍNEZ:

An admirable choice.

FATHER IGNATIUS:

Father Simon should be at Lisbon by now, but Bobadilla is not ready. He cannot go until he is cured of an ague that has seized him, and that same ague has paralysed my plans.

FATHER LAÍNEZ:

Does it not seem, Father, that the Society was fated never to have an easy path?

FATHER IGNATIUS:

That's a sign that it deserves it! You cannot make oil without crushing olives, nor wine without the winepress. That's why—and because harsh winds brace the body—when I pray to God every morning for my Society, I do not ask favours for it; I do not ask for an easy and flowery path through the world. I ask for it—persecution! Aye, and at the same time, pardon for the persecutors.

[*Pause: distant bells begin to be heard, sounding the last hour.* FATHER IGNATIUS *rises.*]

FATHER BROËT:

Bells . . . what is the hour?

FATHER IGNATIUS:

The hour to retire. [*All rise*] Let us pray. . . . [*Silent prayer.*] May God keep us all this night and give us part in His holy Kingdom. . . . My sons, if you do not wish to ask me anything further, I am going within, to write.

FATHER SALMERÓN:

Father Ignatius, I beg you, in God's name, not to rob yourself of so many hours of sleep. Your sight will be injured, and your health.

FATHER IGNATIUS:

Ah, but there are papers that must be dealt with at once. If there were nothing before us but devotions and prayers, visiting hospitals, preaching in the churches, life would be all recreation and pleasure. No, but there is a time for everything, and sometimes the affairs of the messenger boy and the house servant have to be settled between an *Our Father* and a *Hail Mary*. Heaven would be too airy to be real but that the Lord founds even the finest of His works on stone foundations and strengthens them with bonds of steel.

[*He is about to go out, at the left.*]

FATHER LAÍNEZ:

But give us your blessing.

FATHER IGNATIUS:

[*Raising his hand over them*] God keep you all; do not forget me in your prayers.

[*As he is about to go out,* FRANCIS XAVIER *comes in, somewhat precipitately, still in his soutane, by the right. He goes to* FATHER IGNATIUS *and kneels.*]

XAVIER:

Father Ignatius, Father Ignatius; do not go to your room without sparing a wee blessing for me.

FATHER IGNATIUS:

[*Hardly concealing his affection*] The last to come home, and always the first to set forth. . . . [*Blessing him*] Father Francis, may God bless you, and give you Heaven.

[*He goes out.* FATHER XAVIER *has seated himself with signs of exhaustion.*]

FATHER SALMERÓN:

How did you employ the day, Father?

XAVIER:

I attended one stricken by the plague; I heard confessions at St. John's; I got ready some sermons. Och! I could find time for nothing.

FATHER LEFÈVRE:

As if you did nothing!

XAVIER:

Ah, but, Father, one must be more diligent. There is so much—so much to do.

FATHER SALMERÓN:

Has Father Xavier heard the news of the East?

XAVIER:

I only know that Father Ignatius is planning a Mission there, and that he is moving slowly but surely to his purpose. [*Exultant, as he imagines the Mission*] Oh, what a moment that would be: to arrive there and to cry out to those who wait: "Come all ye and listen!" To break, with our accent, the silence of that air which never before heard the words of truth!

FATHER LAÍNEZ:

Do not let your imagination be taken up with fancies.

XAVIER:

And who, then, are they who are to carry the seed to the East?

FATHER LAÍNEZ:

[*With slight asperity*] Father Simón Rodríguez and Bobadilla. Those are the Father's choice.

XAVIER:

[*Repressing an instinictive motion of disappointment*] I am sure that among all the Fathers there could not be found two better fitted for so hard a task. . . . But —only these two?

FATHER LAÍNEZ:

Are you not pleased that only these two are going?

XAVIER:

Nobody ever knows aught of the designs of God.

FATHER LAÍNEZ:

[*With friendly irony*] I think you'd like to burst headlong through those limits of the world, where the mapmakers write in big letters, *Finis Terræ,* the Earth's End. . . .

XAVIER:

[*Vehemently*] Oh, why *Finis Terræ* like a magic charm, forbidding any further endeavour—any further inquiry? He's a timid creature who is bound in and discouraged by those little words. While there's any corner of the earth where He is not adored Who came to save us, the world's end has not been found. [*Overcome again by the thought of it*] This Mission to the East, it intoxicates my imagination. How marvellous it is to carry the seed into those new lands!

FATHER LAÍNEZ:

[*Cutting short the discourse, with light irony*] You speak, of course, of Father Simón Rodríguez and of Bobadilla?

XAVIER:

[*Brought back to himself*] I was imagining a case,

Father Laínez; my deeds, I know, are petty and unworthy; still, the poor imagination is free!

[*A bell sounds.*]

FATHER BROËT:

It is time to retire.

FATHER LAÍNEZ:

I did not think that it was so late. God keep you all.

FATHER LEFÈVRE:

May you, too, be in His keeping.

FATHER BROËT:

And you.

[*All go out except* XAVIER, *who has sat in thought; he rises. He goes to a niche at the right, where an image of Our Lady stands. The little lamp has gone out.* XAVIER *dips a finger to see if the lamp lacks oil.*]

XAVIER:

The lamp has dried up and will not burn. [*He gets oil and puts the lamp right, then gazes on the image for some moments*] My Lady, have compassion on this poor, impetuous fool, who does so little for Your love, yet has such great ambition! I, who but now saw myself in imagination journeying to the Indies, bearing the new and holy seed—it has remained for me just to put oil in Your little lamp! My poor stature does not reach to the great things that I imagined to myself! [*He stays gazing fixidly at the image. His face becomes transfigured. He falls on his knees*] But—You are looking at me? . . . Oh, yes, yes! . . . You fill me with confidence when You look at me like that! [*Pause. As if he converses with Her—softly, humbly.*] As Your Ladyship pleases! [*Another moment he watches Her, breathing hard. Then he lowers his head*] I do not know if I would succeed. I only know that I would do the very best that I could! [*The lay brother enters from the left with a light.* XAVIER *rises, and tries to assume a natural tone*] What do you seek?

THE LAY BROTHER:

The oil jar.

XAVIER:

I have filled the lamp already; and look you—this is how to do it—take note, lest I should not be here. Some day—who knows?—I might be obliged to go on a long journey. . . .

THE LAY BROTHER:

Your Reverence is going to the East, perhaps?

XAVIER:

No. . . . But all the same, mark what I have shewn you in case of anything . . .

[FATHER IGNATIUS *enters by the left, in animated conversation with* DON PEDRO MASCAREÑAS, *the Portuguese Ambassador*]

FATHER IGNATIUS:

The case is urgent. Further delay well might destroy the whole undertaking. We must act accordingly. [*Seeing* XAVIER] Who is that? Ah, God be thanked! We were seeking you. This is my lord the Ambassador, Don Pedro Mascareñas. He has come to tell me that my good son Bobadilla is worse: the ague has taken so bad a turn that it seems imprudent that he should undertake the journey to the East.

MASCAREÑAS:

My letters say not imprudent, but impossible.

XAVIER:

And could not the expedition be delayed a little, to give the Father time to recover?

MASCAREÑAS:

That cannot be done. I am leaving now for Portugal, to join the ships, and I must take with me in my train the missionary, whoever he be, who is to take the Father's place as companion of the good Father Simón Rodríguez.

XAVIER:

It is grievous that the East should lose such a missioner. No one could do the great work better than Nicolás Bobadilla!

FATHER IGNATIUS:

Yet, as I see it, this illness of the Father's is God's clear sign that it is not His will that Bobadilla should go, much as I wished it.

XAVIER:

[*Very timidly*] Then, if that is not His will, Father Ignatius, what *is*?

FATHER IGNATIUS:

As I see it, the Lord has reserved this work for Navarre —and Xavier! [*Pause.* XAVIER *bows his head, saying nothing*] What! Does this news not surprise you?

XAVIER:

I was hoping for it.

FATHER IGNATIUS:

Then why did you not *ask* to be sent?

XAVIER:

If God willed it, what need was there for any little word from me?

MASCAREÑAS:

[*Marvelling*] Do you mean that you are ready to venture your life in a strange and distant world with no more ado than this?

FATHER IGNATIUS:

To him who is ambitious of nothing, all the world is one.

MASCAREÑAS:

When, then, can we set out?

FATHER IGNATIUS:

He'll not be long gathering his baggage, seeing that he possesses no more clothes than you see on him!

XAVIER:

Two minutes will suffice—one, to give thanks to Our Lady, and one to get together my books . . . and to stitch together a tear or two in my soutane.

MASCAREÑAS:

Do you need travelling bags?

XAVIER:

I have them already.

FATHER IGNATIUS:

What then! Did you foresee this?

XAVIER:

Who knows what is in store for him? I prepared for the unexpected! Two evenings back, an old soldier came to the door. He had no money to give as alms, so he made me a present of some bags. I accepted them (with equal courtesy) as repaying his little expenses.

FATHER IGNATIUS:

Xavier, these are signs by which God speaks to us unmistakably. This affair of the East manifestly is reserved for you—yours is the honour of this great undertaking. Now, now, my dear Xavier, you can give free rein in your heart to that unbounded ambition which I have bidden you so often to curb. It needs no longer to be pent up, like water by a dam. It can fly to its mark, that zeal of yours, like an arrow on the wind, that is aimed truly for the target. O my son, there is no fear now that your zeal will be left to fritter itself away! The torrent now has scope enough to swell into a mighty river!

MASCAREÑAS:

Well, then?

XAVIER:

I am in your Excellency's hands.

FATHER IGNATIUS:

[*To the* LAY BROTHER, *who has been standing by*] Brother, summon the Fathers. They must hear the news, and share both the grief and the joy of this moment, as good brethren should.

[*The* LAY BROTHER *goes out by the right.*]

MASCAREÑAS:

Then, God willing, we will start out to-morrow morning. Father Xavier, I would have you come to my house this same night, if it is convenient, so that we can put together supplies for the journey.

XAVIER:

If Father Ignatius does not command otherwise, I will be with you.

[*The* FATHERS, *with the* LAY BROTHER, *enter by the right.*]

FATHER IGNATIUS:

Come, my sons; for I have tidings for you. Father Nicolás is so ill in Naples that he cannot set out for Lisbon for a long time. I have chosen a substitute, so that our Mission can proceed at once; and I have chosen your comrade, Father Xavier.

FATHER SALMERÓN:

[*Embracing him*] Father Xavier!

FATHER BROËT:

[*Doing likewise*] God bless your undertaking.

FATHER LAÍNEZ:

[*The same*] So you got it after all!

XAVIER:

Father Laínez, we folk of Navarre are a dogged lot!

FATHER LEFÈVRE:

Do you remember, Father Xavier, our talks over the map in College? They have come to something, eh?

XAVIER:

Do you mind how often I went over those routes with the pointer that I am going to travel now in body and spirit both?

FATHER LEFÈVRE:

You were the good husbandman. You spied out the field before you went sowing the seed.

[*Face p.* 56

ACT I.—THE FIRST HOUSE OF THE SOCIETY OF JESUS IN ROME

ST. IGNATIUS: I bless you, Xavier, and may God bless your work.

FATHER LAÍNEZ:

And when does the journey begin?

MASCAREÑAS:

We set out in the morning; and Father Xavier honours me by lodging with me to-night.

FATHER LEFÈVRE:

So soon?

FATHER SALMERÓN:

What need for so much haste?

FATHER IGNATIUS:

It is best so. It is best for emotion to be cut short. When great resolutions are taken, they will succeed all the better if we attack them at once and go through with them with decision.

MASCAREÑAS:

Well then, if there is nothing else? . . .

XAVIER:

[*Kneeling before* FATHER IGNATIUS] I ask only for your blessing and your counsel, before I go.

FATHER IGNATIUS:

I bless you, Xavier, and may God bless your works! [*Pause. He raises his eyes for a moment to Heaven*] You are going forth on a mighty undertaking. There is one great danger: that you may be so carried away in the zeal of your labours that you may forget that which is your concern within. Mark you: the interior life is of more consequence than external works. No deed is worth anything unless it grows out of the spirit —out of love. In the midst of other matters, think chiefly of the inner things. It is the heart of the rose that holds together the petals.

Every day beg God to send you slights and humiliations; for glory—even if it were glory won in Christ's service—I fear it. Go not to rest any night without some moments' meditation on death and judgment; for, as I think, it is better to sleep upon these harsh and ugly thoughts than to lay your head on a pillow of wood or stone.

Every morning, talk for a little while with Our Lady. Tell to Her those sad secrets which one can tell more easily to Her than to our Heavenly Father, seeing that we fear Him more. From time to time, mix into your work little ejaculations—offer up some little mental prayer; these will perfume your toil, like incense. Let not prayer impede work, nor work prayer. Weaving together sally rods and rushes, we can fashion at the one time a wicker-basket for the earth and a Rosary for Heaven.

Write to me minutely, telling me of your doings and your fortunes. Do not magnify your deeds through vanity, nor minimize them through modesty; for the glory of them will belong to God—the errors are all yours.

[*With deep emotion, laying his hands on* XAVIER'S *head*]

I think that, in this life, we two never will see each other again. For you, I entreat that salvation which I desire for us both, through God's goodness, and not through any merit of our own. Meanwhile and always, O my dear Xavier, bear me within your heart, even as I ever will bear you in mine.

XAVIER:

[*He rises, full of emotion, and dries a tear*] Forgive me, Father Ignatius, that I do not speak what I feel. You, who understand souls so well, you can interpret my silence. Have you not taught me, by lesson and example, that speech is most brief when feeling is most strong? [*He embraces the other* FATHERS.] Brothers, never forget Xavier in your prayers.

MASCAREÑAS:

Come now, let us be off, or you'll see an ambassador howling like a child!

XAVIER:

I beg you all . . .

MASCAREÑAS:

I am sorry for the discomfort of the journey that's before us. Through all Rome, my servants could get no more than three mules fit to ride, and one lame beast.

XAVIER:

I claim the lame one first! I have spoken first, and none can take away my right to it!

MASCAREÑAS:

A soldier of Navarre off to the wars on a lame mule—what?

XAVIER:

I will not give up my claim. Father Ignatius, you know, is for ever rebuking my fiery impatience. I am thinking that we'll be well matched, that mule and I; for when I spur on, he'll draw back. [*He seizes* MASCAREÑAS *by the arm; speaks from the door*] Come then! Comrades, you see a lame mule setting off for the Indies. So, step by step, helping one another, we will go—to cure at once my mule's lameness, and this galloping ambition of mine.

[*He goes out with* MASCAREÑAS.]

[CURTAIN]

ACT II

SCENE I

An apartment in the Royal Palace at Lisbon. A door at the left; another, curtained, at the right. Seated on cushioned chairs in an alcove, DON MARTIN ALONSO DE SOUSA, *the* COUNT DE CASTAÑEDA, DON ALVARO DE ATAYDE, *the ambassador* MASCAREÑAS, and a LADY.

DON MARTIN

All is ready. The ship is laden and provisioned. The crew is aboard. This very day we can raise anchor for the Indies.

CASTAÑEDA:

I hear that the two Fathers of the new Company, who are going to the East, will be received in audience by his Majesty this afternoon.

DON MARTIN

So it is said; but it seems that the King wishes them to remain in Lisbon instead of going to the Indies.

MASCAREÑAS:

Aye, but it is said, too, that Prince Henry, the King's son, is opposed to this. He holds that the Court ought not to deny this blessing to the Indies; here, the Fathers are not needed as they are needed yonder—missionaries to preach the Faith.

THE LADY:

All the same, I do hope that the Fathers will remain at Court.

ATAYDE:

That is what all the ladies are saying; they follow the Fathers like so many children. There's nothing, Count, but visits to the chapel and running from church to church — "Who is preaching?" — "When will the Stations be said?"—"Which of the Fathers says Mass?" —Oh, but this is a poor year for the gallants, this year of prayers and sermons and devotions!

CASTAÑEDA:

That is as may be, here in the Palace, where the soil is harder than it is out yonder in the town. The simpler the soil, the better it takes the seed. The churches in the suburbs are crowded out when the Fathers preach; the day is not long enough for them to hear confessions. When they go out into the streets after devotions or Mass, the little lads of the gutter follow them, and the little girls strew their way with flowers. The quays and promenades are not the places that we used to know, schools for buffoons and pickpockets. Merchants trade honestly now, bonds are honoured and promises are kept. In a word, and I care not who denies it, 'tis the truth itself, Lisbon that was known for fights and thefts and all manner of rascality, is itself no more; it is turned inside out, like a silk stocking!

ATAYDE:

Not more so than the Court. The King thinks so much of them that he's ready to oblige them by making us all monks.

THE LADY:

They say that he has signed a decree ordering all his pages to go to Confession every week.

ATAYDE:

I knew this Ignatius and his friends, his Company as they are now, in Paris. I tell you that the world has to change itself wherever they appear.

MASCAREÑAS:

I can tell you wonders of this Father who came with me from Rome. When we were riding through Navarre on the way to Portugal, we passed almost by the very gate of the Castle of Xavier, where his mother still lives. I offered to halt our little caravan for just an hour or two, so that he could go and bid farewell to her, seeing that it's likely he never will see her alive again. What did he answer? "Eternity", said he, "will be very long, and just now we are in a hurry," and he spurred on the lame mule that had carried him from Rome. But I saw, Atayde, when the sun was setting—I saw its light sparkle on something on his face. Very simply he said to me, "It is only the wind that has made my eyes water a little."

ATAYDE:

Oh, I don't doubt that they are Saints . . . only, these Saints bore one, sometimes!

THE LADY:

Yet, you are for ever in his company, Atayde.

ATAYDE:

My dear girl, necessity commands, business obliges! I go walking after him because I want him to ask his

Majesty for something for me, which his Majesty will grant him, though I might save my breath.

THE LADY:

And what is it?

ATAYDE:

A licence enabling me to go to the Indies.

DON MARTIN

What, do you, too, wish to go there?

ATAYDE:

I, too, Don Martín; for I hear great tidings of the opportunities that abound there. Load up five ships with spices and cloves, and, given a fair voyage and a good price, there's a fortune made without anxiety or toil. Look at Juan Freytas: he was two years in the Indies; he used to go dressed in home-spun, now he goes in silk.

MASCAREÑAS:

And you are asking Father Xavier's help in this affair?

ATAYDE:

I am relying on our old friendship and companionship in Paris. It is hard, very hard, to get a licence, that is well known; but if he asks it——

[*A* PAGE *enters by the right.*]

PAGE:

[*Addressing* COUNT CASTAÑEDA] Sir, the Fathers have arrived for the audience that has been promised.

CASTAÑEDA:

Let their Reverences come this way.

THE LADY:

What luck!

[*The* PAGE *raises the curtain to let pass* FATHER SIMÓN RODRÍGUEZ *and* FATHER FRANCIS XAVIER.]

MASCAREÑAS:

[*Announcing them*] Father Simón and Father Xavier.

[*The* FATHERS *bow to the group.*]

XAVIER:

There was no delay in admitting us.

CASTAÑEDA:

The King is all afire to see your Reverences; it will be a wonder if he does not go on his knees to you.

THE LADY:

[*To* XAVIER, *with extravagant flattery*] Before your Reverence every eye must sparkle, every face must bow. . . .

XAVIER:

[*Sharply*] And every dog must bark.

THE LADY:

If his Majesty decides that you must leave to morrow, won't you give me a little clipping from your soutane?

XAVIER:

This is a foolish custom that has come into practice among women, to sew scraps of a Friar's habit in their scarves.

THE LADY:

These are just signs of our admiration.

XAVIER:

You'd do better to carry our counsels in your hearts.

It is vain to listen to sermons, to go to Mass and prayers, unless your daily life conforms with all this devotion. My Lady, you will find my confessional in the cathedral.

THE LADY:

[*Somewhat piqued*] Oh, a thousand thanks!

XAVIER:

[*Retiring*] At your feet!

ATAYDE:

This bluntness and plain speaking amount almost to arrogance.

XAVIER:

[*Turning*] Oh, pardon!—but you see, sometimes I remember that I come from rough Navarre!—And you?

ATAYDE:

It is all in your hands, Father Xavier, whether I go to the East.

XAVIER:

Very good, my brother; but tell me, do you go as a Christian, or as a trader? Mark you, if I have the decision, no one shall go over the ocean to discredit Christ among the negroes.

DON MARTIN

[*Who has overheard them and approaches*] When you have more knowledge of the negroes, Father, this enthusiasm of yours will cool. You will find that they are fit for little more than a slave's task in our galleys. They are not worth notice save as likely captives for the oars.

XAVIER:

By these overbearing, these tyrannical ways, what the Missionaries do, the Viceroys undo.

DON MARTIN

Och, what are they but miserable pagans, with no religion?

XAVIER:

What are they? Why, by the natural law, our brothers! There are some Christians of whom one hardly can say the same. Those poor creatures live according to their instincts, like unbroken colts. They can make and they can kill: what they do not know how to do is how to be half good and half bad, like some of you! I am going out to baptize them that they may be better than they are; and I'd baptize you with these hands in like manner if there were another baptism for bad Christians.

DON MARTIN:

You preach a plain sermon.

XAVIER:

Clear water and pure wine.

ATAYDE:

And the usual tincture of arrogance!

XAVIER:

Oh, I can be polite with honest ignorance; but your half-and-half people may look for bluntness when I speak.

THE LADY:

[*As the voices are raised*] Hush, hush, or this talk will not end as it began.

DON MARTIN

[*Somewhat vexed*] Will we be going?

CASTAÑEDA:

I have to go to prepare for his Majesty's visit.

[*They go out by the left.*]

FATHER SIMON

[*Who had stood apart*] This has been somewhat unpleasant. . . .

XAVIER:

Maybe, Father; but look you—there is so much to be done that I have no time, on top of everything else, to be . . . prudent!

[ATAYDE, *who has gone out with the others, returns to* XAVIER.]

ATAYDE:

Xavier, the King is coming almost at once for the audience. You'll ask him for the licence?

XAVIER:

Are you resolved, Atayde, to amend your errors and wrong-doing?—for if you do not change we will be enemies and opponents still, as in Paris.

ATAYDE:

I promise you, Father, to be better henceforward than I have been hitherto.

[DOÑA LEONOR DE ARIZA, *the Queen's lady, enters from the right, with covered face.*]

DOÑA LEONOR:

Is Father Xavier here?

XAVIER:

Raise your veil, Señora.

[*She raises it.* ATAYDE *starts.*]

DOÑA LEONOR:

Atayde!

ATAYDE:

So you have found me, Leonor!

DOÑA LEONOR:

I came seeking the Father, but the Lord brought you here without my seeking: you can hear my words, too. Father, I know how you attend to the sorrows of others, and I have come to tell you mine.

ATAYDE:

He is engaged with the King; he cannot listen to you now.

XAVIER:

I always listen to those who need me. Who are you?

DOÑA LEONOR:

I am Leonor de Ariza, a lady of the Queen's; this man, wooing me with his honeyed words, promised me marriage, but now he would cast me aside like a plume from his hat.

ATAYDE:

You are making a false case.

DOÑA LEONOR:

Where have I spoken falsely?

ATAYDE:

You will not take me like a bird in a net. You pressed yourself on me; I did not woo you. I owe you nothing. Is not that so, Xavier?

XAVIER:

Your defence condemns you. . . . I begin to see now why you are eager to be off to the Indies. When I knew you of old, you had some conscience: but now, no!—you would make me your accomplice. Xavier is not so simple as you think. If you want that licence, you must pay its price. You must keep your promise and marry this lady.

ATAYDE:

What's that you say?

XAVIER:

[*With energy*] That you'll not go on with your plans and ambitions unless you redeem your word. You may work out your perdition yet in some other way, but not in this. The King demands honour in his people; if I tell all, maybe it's not to the East you'll go, but to prison.

ATAYDE:

I promise, then, that when I come back from the East. . . .

XAVIER:

Before you sail, the marriage must be!

PAGE:

[*Opening the curtain at the left*] The King!

XAVIER:

[*Hurriedly showing* LEONOR *and* ATAYDE *into a room at the right*] You two must not be here. [*To* ATAYDE] You know your duty now.

ATAYDE:

But you must promise me the licence!

XAVIER:

You shall have it. [*The* KING *enters by the left, followed by* CASTAÑEDA.] May the Lord give you peace!

THE KING:

And may He bless you, Xavier! [*He sits. The* COUNT *behind him; the* FATHERS *stand before him.*] You know, Fathers, I am sure, that I have been asked and implored, here in the Palace, to keep you here. I have consulted Father Ignatius by letter; and, by his advice, this is what we will do: Father Rodríguez will remain at Our Court, and you, Xavier, will go to the Indies alone.

FATHER SIMON:

I know well that the Indies do not need me, but I am sorry that this is why I must stay behind.

XAVIER:

God asks it of you, for His love; there is nothing but to obey. Sometimes, not to go out to hardship, because it grieves you more to be spared it, has more merit in the Lord's eyes.

THE KING:

How generously these Brethren take all that comes!

XAVIER:

Our little human wishes, what are they beside the designs of God? . . . Ever since I was a child, I have heard a voice that calls me to the East. . . . And now, we are face to face, the East and I, as in a duel! This morning, walking by the quays, I stood, and saw the galleon riding on the waters, snug and taut; and I thought that her tapering mast was like a pen, that is to write my destiny.

Oh, but I was overcome!—the light, the vessels on the sea, the glory of the sunny morning, bright with joy—and then the long road of the ocean that lies before our ship, leading on, on, on to distant lands and peoples! I trembled like a hound on the leash.

THE KING:

Father Francis, this surely proves, over and above all else, that it is God who chose you for this work, seeing how the task agrees with your desire—your vocation.

XAVIER:

God grant that it be so; I unite my will to His.

THE KING:

And I will be behind you, I will be your aid; God gives the sceptre to kings that they should use it to promote the Faith. I do desire to see the Cross set high in my realm of the Indies. To this end, then, you must give me faithful reports, so that I may do all that is needed to correct what you find wrong; you must tell me of my people's spiritual state, the number and proportion of the Faithful and of infidels; where the Faith is well-served, and where Christ is neglected—His light untended, or His teaching disobeyed. . . . I would not have a Crown that was not crowned by the Cross!

XAVIER:

There is no government for any people so good as the fatherly rule of a wise and Christian King. All other ways are vain; judgments can err, and laws can be unjust. A man and a nation can ask for nothing better than a good father and a good King.

THE KING:

I thank you, Father Xavier, for your words. This King

would only wish to be that which you think him to be! [*To* CASTAÑEDA] Count, the voyage will be long; you must make ample provision.

XAVIER:

My person and my dream—they're all the load I carry!

CASTAÑEDA:

Surely you should take some page from the Court.

XAVIER:

You need not be concerned with anything further, for me. I have my cross, my Rosary, and my scapular on my shoulders to defend me.

CASTAÑEDA:

We are not seeking more martyrs, that any of the expedition should go out unprotected. Who will protect your life?

XAVIER:

He who protects the roses and the lilies! Meanwhile, the poorer and the simpler the life, the greater the peace of it. I have more than enough. But look you, I am taking with me Mansilla, the lay Brother.

THE KING:

Forget not, Xavier, that you have been appointed Nuncio of all the East.

CASTAÑEDA:

And in such a rank, such a dignity, it is but proper to take a man servant to dress you and perform your toilet.

XAVIER:

Count, you'll set me laughing with such solemn reasons! You'd be surprised if you knew how well I can dress myself!—But have no fear for the Nunciature. In a stable, in Bethlehem, slept Christ, who is our All, and a Nuncio is but His servant and representative.

THE KING:

Why do you press your offers, Count, seeing that he declines them all?

CASTAÑEDA:

I only wish to serve him. . . .

THE KING:

Our human counsels, and all our prudence, are trivial beside his divine undertaking. To-morrow morning at sunrise, if may be, the ships must weigh anchor, and sail for the East, with Xavier. . . . [*To* XAVIER] And remember, Father, as you travel on this Mission which you have desired so much, Portugal's wishes go with you; when the ships shatter the crystal of the seas, our prayers will be with the winds that bend the sails. [*To* FATHER SIMÓN] . . . And you, Father, do not be angry with us. Bear you in mind that you are to be the compass and the North Star of my Kingdom and my Court, even as Xavier of the East. [*Rising*] . . . Go you in peace, Father Xavier!

XAVIER:

First pardon me, Lord King, that I beg of you one parting favour.

THE KING:

What shall it be?

XAVIER:

[*To* CASTAÑEDA] Count: if the King allows it, summon

Atayde and a certain lady to the presence ; they are here together, at my invitation.

THE KING:

I wish to please you in all things. Let them enter.

[*The* COUNT *brings* ATAYDE *and* DOÑA LEONOR *from the right, where they bow.* XAVIER *takes* ATAYDE *by the hand and leads him alone to the* KING.]

THE COUNT:

Come, both of you.

ATAYDE:

Thanks, Count.

XAVIER:

This is Atayde, Señor, whom I love—and he loves me. He was my best friend in Paris, when I was young ; we studied together. *If ever we differed, it was over matters of affection.* He wishes to go to the East with me, and I ask your Majesty for the licence, that he may come to-morrow.

THE KING:

He intends to trade in spices?

ATAYDE:

I hope to succeed in that business.

THE KING:

Every day there are plenty who make the same request, but not all of them have a Xavier for a sponsor. [*To* CASTAÑEDA] . . . Tell my secretary to prepare the necessary papers.

ATAYDE:

Señor, this is an immense favour!

THE KING:

And this lady?

XAVIER:

[*Drawing* LEONOR *to the* KING] Raise now your face without fear. This is a Lady of the Queen's; Atayde is her betrothed husband. He wishes to ask your Majesty —*for he is very earnest in this matter*—leave to cut short the formalities, and to marry her in the morning.

THE KING:

Aye, and she can travel with him to the East.

XAVIER:

With this, you have filled to overflowing your kindness —and Atayde's happiness; *and now can the wife follow the husband, and be his guide! He wished to ask for this, but he dared not.* [*To* ATAYDE] This was quick work, eh, Atayde?

ATAYDE:

Very quick. . . .

XAVIER:

[*To* LEONOR] Señora, for this happiness, return your thanks to the King.

DOÑA LEONOR:

[*Lowering her face*] I do not know how to speak what I feel.

THE KING:

[*Rising*] Is that all?

XAVIER:

All, save to kiss your Majesty's hands.

DOÑA LEONOR:

We too. [ATAYDE *and* LEONOR *kiss the* KING'S *hands*]

THE KING:

[*To* XAVIER] And now—to win more Christians for Christ! I will see you before you sail. . . . May your Mission be as the Lord desires, and may He be glorified in all!

XAVIER:

And may He lengthen the days of a King who uses them so well!

[*The* KING *goes out at the left, followed by the* COUNT.]

ATAYDE:

[*Who only waited for the* KING'S *departure to approach* XAVIER, *angrily*] You forgot nothing when you spoke for me!

XAVIER:

God willed that I should speak so; and mark you, what I said, if it was not strictly true, see that you make it so. If I spoke for you, it was through charity. What I said here, you must make good: not for Xavier, not for my sake, but for your own . . . and for the sake of JESUS: Him whose light you have refused to see, Him whom you are for ever nailing to the Cross anew. You will try?

ATAYDE:

[*Touched, yet struggling against grace*] Yes, yes, Xavier. . . . But a servant and a wife are much to take on so long a voyage.

XAVIER:

Do not speak with the meanness of a merchant. . . . I tell you, Atayde, that I rejoice now that I am taking you with me. So will the enemy battle against a double defence; aye, and I will have at hand more souls to win!

ATAYDE:

You judge me like a heathen.

XAVIER:

I am sorry that it is needed, and I have no wish to vex you.

ATAYDE:

[*In open anger*] Oh, if it were not for the favour that you have done me!

XAVIER:

Spit out of your conscience that hatred which is fermenting in it. Have no fear for your licence; it is not in danger. . . . I want you for my companion just because you were sent by God for that; I will bear you with me as close as haircloth to the skin.

[*Hurriedly, from the right, enter* DON MARTIN, *with* MASCAREÑAS *and two* LADIES. *As the curtain parts, other* LADIES *and* COURTIERS *are seen talking, excitedly in the adjoining chamber.*]

MASCAREÑAS:

Come, come, Father Xavier!

XAVIER:

What is happening?

MASCAREÑAS:

The news is going round that you are about to sail, and all the courtiers wish to see you and to kiss your hands.

XAVIER:

My hands!

FIRST LADY:

Because the Father is leaving so soon and going so far.

XAVIER:

[*Drily*] If what they want is my farewell counsels, it is well.

SECOND LADY:

Is it certain, then, that you are going?

XAVIER:

And Atayde goes with me. Right glad I am to have so good a friend as companion.

ATAYDE:

And I the same!

XAVIER:

[*Presenting* DOÑA LEONOR] And Atayde's wife also is coming.

FIRST LADY:

Can it be?

SECOND LADY:

How quiet Don Alvaro kept the match!

XAVIER:

To-morrow, at daybreak, the marriage will be celebrated. . . .

MASCAREÑAS:

Swift notice!

[*Enter* CASTAÑEDA *by the right.*]

CASTAÑEDA:

They will not be satisfied, Father; they are crowding the hall, awaiting you; and in the Square the people are gathering, hoping for your blessing. You can go up to the balcony and shew yourself to the throng; they are impatient.

XAVIER:

Not more impatient than I, Castañeda, to leave these halls and chambers and to be away among the Indians, in the East! [*Resigned*] Well, let us go, as you wish.

FIRST LADY:

[*Kissing his hand*] Do not refuse me your hand!

SECOND LADY:

[*Bending to kiss his soutane*] The sun will rise on the Indies when you arrive there with your Mission.

XAVIER:

[*Halting, with a sudden inspiration*] Señora: what beautiful jewels you have!

SECOND LADY:

[*Alarmed a little*] Do you want them from me?

XAVIER:

No; but it came to my mind that there is an old woman down in the poor streets, dying; she has no clothing, no food in the house.

SECOND LADY:

I will send a servant with alms.

XAVIER:

She lives just behind the church . . . and listen: if

ACT II.—IN THE ROYAL PALACE AT LISBON

[Face p. 80

ST. FRANCIS XAVIER: What beautiful jewels you have, my lady!

only your Ladyship would go in person, it would be the greatest charity of all.

SECOND LADY:

I will go.

XAVIER:

Oh, but it will cheer her, if you only set your foot in her little dwelling. . . . And that, Señora, is my Last Will! [*He steps towards the hall.*]

MASCAREÑAS:

In a bare hour you have roused up the indifferent folk and set them by the ears; you have begged alms and benefits; you have made a match . . .

XAVIER:

Oh, and pardon me, Señora, if I was a trifle harsh in speech, in my haste—and forgot to smile politely. I am more the friend of the rough winds, my lady, than of the summery breezes. . . . Aye, one must seize the chance and do good in a hurry; for evil never loses a moment!

[*He goes out into the hall, the* COURTIERS *swarming on him to kiss his hands and his soutane.*]

[CURTAIN]

ACT II

SCENE II

Malacca. Bamboo huts at the entrance to a village; palm trees in the centre, in the shadow of which, seated on stones, are MANSILLA, *the Lay Brother;* FATHER COSME DE TORRES, *a Portuguese priest; and* MATTHEW, *a black convert. The Europeans talk;* MATTHEW, *eating fruit, listens, with gestures of surprise.*

FATHER COSME:

So, arriving at last in the East, the Father leapt ashore . . .

MANSILLA:

Yes, at Goa, our Indian city; and you know that Goa is another Lisbon for liveliness and riches. From there, Father Xavier went preaching throughout the fishing quarters; days and nights were one to him, always working for Christ.

FATHER COSME:

Does he purpose to return to Goa?

MANSILLA:

Yes, surely; but he wishes first to preach here in Malacca. It is not wise to rest long in Goa. . . . Ah, but this East, this East, is treacherous; it does not make open war on a man, but it soothes him and betrays him, with its perfumes and its ease. We from the West are assailed by sweet nothings, the mind is lulled to idleness by its delights, and our purpose is wooed from us.

FATHER COSME:

There is a mighty harvest here in Malacca awaiting his sickle.

MANSILLA:

Aye, and what is more, there are less tares to swallow up the good grain.

FATHER COSME:

What do you mean by tares?

MANSILLA:

I mean this: that the very dregs of Portugal are emptied over there, in Goa. It is these who stand in the way of Christ and His witness. Every miserable Portuguese, who is but a rascally adventurer in his own country, puts on the marquis when he doubles the Cape. These self-made gentry bear themselves so cruelly, so contemptuously, towards the poor unbelievers that no mission can prevail against their vile example. What is the use of preaching of Christian love in the church, if the very opposite is what Christians display? There are some of these traders who lash their dark servants—lash them, and count the blows on a Rosary!

FATHER COSME:

Yes, the Father will be better here, in this unspoilt place, than yonder in that hotbed of commerce, among traders who have neither conscience nor fear of God. . . .

[*A sound of bells in the distance.*]

VOICES OF CHILDREN [*afar off*]:

[*In solemn music, answering the bells.*]

The Virgin Mary knelt one day
(Holy Mary!) praying;
And by the door the Angel came
Shining in white, and saying:

XAVIER'S VOICE:

[*Afar off*] A little alms, brothers, a little gift!—Don't make me ask for it! Help, help, to bring to Christ new Christians!

[*The bell rings, nearer and nearer.*]

FATHER COSME:

It is Father Xavier!

MANSILLA:

Himself!—here he comes, begging his way, with the children about him as always—singing little verses in which he teaches them the catechism.

VOICES OF CHILDREN [*nearer*]:

Hail, O Mary, full of grace
(He said in adoration)—
Blessed are You among women all
And Your Son's incarnation. . . .

FATHER COSME:

What lovely, golden voices!

FATHER XAVIER'S VOICE:

[*Very near*] A little alms, brothers, a little gift, for the new Christians!

MANSILLA:

The choir of voices draws near.

FATHER COSME:

Look! I see his habit.

MATTHEW:

Even so, in the forest at the break of day, the birds break into song to tell us morning's come.

[FATHER XAVIER *enters from the right, in a dirty and torn soutane; a little bell in his hand. Children, black and brown, surround him. He dismisses the children, giving them his hands to kiss.*]

XAVIER:

And now, my lads, away home with you!—and be careful in your play!—and remember all that I have taught you!

—Ah, Mansilla, and did you visit that old woman?

MANSILLA:

I went twice.

XAVIER:

And you, Matthew, did you go to Juan de Aranjo, for his wine?

MATTHEW:

The mean fellow foresaw that you would ask it. He said—and I don't believe him—that he had so little that he could spare none. . . .

XAVIER:

The foolish fellow! You must tell him, Matthew, that I bid him to change his ways. . . . [*For a moment he is still, gazing into vacancy, as if inspired.*] Aye, change his ways, in God's name, and prepare himself: for within five days they will bear him to his burial. . . . It is stupid economy to hoard up his wine. . . . he cannot take it with him.

[*He makes to sit on the stones, exhausted.*]

FATHER COSME:

Come, Father, and rest yourself.

MANSILLA:

Going through the brambles, you have torn your soutane to tatters. . . . Have you pain?

XAVIER:

My arms ache. . . .

MANSILLA:

Your arms?

XAVIER:

With baptizing.

FATHER COSME:

You had many baptisms, then?

XAVIER:

Hundreds came and begged me to baptize their children, and to preach.

FATHER COSME:

And you preached?

XAVIER:

Just the Commandments—in a clearing in the forest. I cannot remember that I ever saw a better church; there was no echo, not a syllable was lost. Oh, what a pulpit is a tree-trunk, with a sounding-board over your head of green leaves!

MANSILLA:

Are you pleased, Father?

XAVIER:

So-so! I only wish that more were done. If only there

were more workers, what a vineyard this would be for good wine! When I think how much my poor weak hands have reaped, I hope for greater things. I will call these islands of Meliapur and Malacca the Islands of Hope in God.

MATTHEW:

[*Exclaiming*] Oh, may I be always beside you, Father! I know that the gate will be opened when you reach it, and so will I get inside!

XAVIER:

It may rather be the other way, Matthew. When you arrive, they'll fling the doors wide open; and may I profit by your entrance to slip in, too!

MANSILLA:

Do you see what he means? Does your mind grasp it? [*To* MATTHEW.]

MATTHEW:

[*Humbly*] The music of a river, gently murmuring, is sweet, though you cannot make words of it; and when Father Xavier speaks, I would not try to explain what he says; yet his clear, kind voice is like a river that sings to me of the things of God.

FATHER COSME:

What things he says!

XAVIER:

And he speaks truly. In how many souls the seed of faith lies, waiting only to be called to flower!

FATHER COSME:

Yes, Father, every day I see it more clearly—these mountains and plains, as I believe, are full of Christians, baptized by desire.

MANSILLA:

What a consolation to think that if they do not know the truth, at least they reverence it!

XAVIER:

And for me, what a responsibility! . . If tradition does not err, brothers, these people once upon a time were Christians.

MANSILLA:

How so, Father?

XAVIER:

In ancient times St. Thomas—that Disciple who was not content even with the sight of the wounded side of Christ but must fortify his faith by touching the wound —St. Thomas, according to tradition, came to evangelize this kingdom, and by his deeds won pardon for his doubts. It is said that he dwelt in an open hut, of coarse poles, surrounded by a band of splendid peacocks. Sometimes, overcome by the fervour of love, he would lash himself with the discipline of thorns; and the peacocks, opening wide their brilliant plumage, hid his devotion from all earthly eyes. One day, one quiet, sunny day, a hunter passed; he saw the plumage and never guessed that Thomas was behind it; he loosed an arrow, and behold you!—it sped into the side of the good saint, who died, happy in his agony, and full of love and heavenly consolation, thinking of the like wound in the Saviour's own precious body.

MANSILLA:

Truly, the soil that was ploughed up so thoroughly before our days was well prepared for the seed.

XAVIER:

[*Rising*] Aye. . . . And enough now of talk; for the time that we let pass in talk, we never can regain. [*To* MATTHEW] You have to ring the bell for the Rosary.

[MATTHEW *goes out at the right, followed by* MANSILLA; ATAYDE *comes in at the left, followed by negroes bearing burdens—they pass over, but he remains.*]

ATAYDE:

God save you!

[*He walks swiftly, as if to enter the village, at the right.*]

XAVIER:

[*Detaining him with a gesture*] Where goes Atayde with so much haste? Is he so pressed with business that he has not a moment left to talk with friends in the shadow of the palms?

ATAYDE:

Business! It would be a fine way of business to follow your directions—as if the niggers would work without one's being after them always; aye, as if one only needed loving words to manage Indians. I tell you, Father Xavier, that money's not caught with honey, like mosquitoes.

XAVIER:

What, then . . . With what? With snares and traps?

ATAYDE:

Business is one thing; holy doings are another.

XAVIER:

But God is only one, and He alone is our Master!

ATAYDE:

[*Evasively*] God. . . .

XAVIER:

God is very distant, very far away on the heights, is that it, Atayde? Ah, but every instant that passes brings you an instant nearer to meeting him: that meeting will be the great moment.—But let us leave this matter; for the water of the fountain plays for ages on the stone, and the stone is so strong that it hardly shows the trace. . . . And now; our own little business?

ATAYDE:

What business? This new notion that you have got into your head, to go and preach a Mission in Macassar, too?

XAVIER:

[*Turning to* FATHER COSME] Look you, Father; is not my request a fair one? The Kingdom of Macassar away down yonder does not retain the smallest trace of the Faith. Some time ago a Portuguese missionary to Malacca, Father Vicente Vegas, went there to preach the Faith, and the old folk tell that he did grand work; his harvest was not mighty but it was not mean. Since then, however, every trace of Christ has been lost there; and is it not just that Atayde, who is so friendly with those Indians, and goes among them trading for cargoes of spices, should grant me the means to go there, too?

ATAYDE:

I am against it, Father, for Macassar is dangerous country, and the people are a bad lot. I would not like—since I love him so dearly—I would not like to lead Father Xavier into such deadly perils.

XAVIER:

Oh, what unhoped-for affection, what tender foresight . . . and so strange! Don Alvaro loves me so much that he loves not that I should move or do my work, or preach. . . .

ATAYDE:

It is only that the voyage thither is over such wild seas, and I would not expose the person of one who labours so mightily for Christ. . . .

XAVIER:

A right way to protect holy things! To check sacrilege, have no procession; and in order not to annoy and excite the evil, do not let them see the good! [*Abandoning restraint*] Aye, and in order that a merchant should have a free hand in his hard dealings for spices and the like, loading his Indians with burden on burden till they faint, it is better that such lands should be left without a missionary: poor fellow, they might turn upon him in their wrath! Perhaps you fear rather that those poor folk, after hearing what he has to say, would not so easily bend their backs to the lash, like dogs, or like beasts of burden to your loads!

ATAYDE:

[*Confused*] It's not that, Father. . . .

XAVIER:

It is not that: no, but it is this—that He whom Judas

once sold for thirty pieces of silver is still made merchandise; every day, He is bought and sold afresh!

ATAYDE:

No, no, Father . . . and you shall see that your suspicions are mistaken. I promise you that when these rains that flood the roads are over, I will see to it that you have means to carry your work to Macassar.

XAVIER:

[*Panting*] You promise, you promise? Look you, Atayde, it galls me to rest while I know that so many souls are waiting for God's light. Look you, my soul is parched with desire; like a stone on the dry beach, or a reed beside the river, I am dying of thirst, being so near the water that I cannot reach.

ATAYDE:

You shall go to Macassar, Father.

[*A bell is sounding.*]

XAVIER:

The Rosary. . . . Can you not spare the time to come with us? . . . To-day I am going to preach on the parable of the rich man, Dives. . . .

ATAYDE:

Are you pointing at anyone?

XAVIER:

Oh, no. The Gospel is for all. I just send forth the holy words like birds, and let them find the branch where they can rest! [*Returning and taking his arm.*] Do not spend the Rosary time in light chatter with evil-livers, down yonder in the town. Remember Doña Leonor, your gracious and beautiful lady.

ATAYDE:

That is enough of that.

XAVIER:

Think now; do nothing but what you would do if eternity started to-morrow. You do not need these base companions, Atayde. All of them together could not save you, but few would be enough to ruin you.

MATTHEW:

[*Entering at right*] Father Xavier, we are ready for the Rosary; but first, if you are not too weary, there is a woman calling for your help.

XAVIER:

What has happened?

MATTHEW:

Her little boy has died.

XAVIER:

And what does she wish?

MATTHEW:

She wants your Reverence to come and read the prayers. . . .

XAVIER:

Come, then, come. One must be doctor here for bodies and souls both.

[*He goes out with* MATTHEW, *at the right.* ATAYDE *is going, when his wife,* DOÑA LEONOR, *enters at the left, followed by a negress who carries a parasol.*]

ATAYDE:

Where is my lady, Doña Leonor, going?

DOÑA LEONOR:

To the Rosary; it is time.

ATAYDE:

Always praying; a good use for your good looks!

DOÑA LEONOR:

[*With sad irony*] You mean that I spend in praying the hours that my husband would like me to spend with him?

ATAYDE:

My time is taken up with work. Why are you complaining? What more do you want? Is there any woman here in Malacca who can envy you? Have you not garments of silk and fine satin?

DOÑA LEONOR:

You remind me of that singing bird that was sad, and its master said, Have you not a golden cage? Ah, but a heart that is injured will be sad, though it be imprisoned in riches.

ATAYDE:

Sad, for what?

DOÑA LEONOR:

Sad for that love which passes me by, though it is mine, as a river that flows past. . . . I know of your wasted hours, and though you see me now with calm eyes, my silence is full of secret tears.

ATAYDE:

Oh, leave me in peace.

DOÑA LEONOR:

What evil has you in its mesh? Accursed be this East,

where evil is in the air, and luxury and ease undo mankind!

ATAYDE:

A woman's nonsense! You have learnt your lesson well from Father Xavier; you see evil everywhere. Could not the holy man find some better way to kill his time?

DOÑA LEONOR:

A saint is always out of favour with a sinner. I can understand that Father Xavier does not please a merchant who drives cruel bargains and misuses the negroes; but as for an unhappy woman, neglected and scorned, his voice that speaks of Heaven is the only consolation left to her in this life.

ATAYDE:

[*Mysteriously*] If that's the way, your comfort will not last long.

DOÑA LEONOR:

What's that?—What do you mean?

ATAYDE:

Why, his Reverence is carrying the Mission to Macassar.

DOÑA LEONOR:

[*Disquieted*] You meant more than that!

ATAYDE:

[*Disturbed*] Woman, what are you hinting?

DOÑA LEONOR:

I have seen strange folk going in and out; I suspect that there is something afoot that you are hiding from me.

ATAYDE:

What are you saying?

DOÑA LEONOR:

You are plotting something against the Father!

ATAYDE:

A woman's nonsense, I say!

DOÑA LEONOR:

When I was out of the house these days, you received an Indian in secret. . . .

ATAYDE:

I was selling him embroideries. . . .

DOÑA LEONOR:

[*Clasping his face and gazing in his eyes*] Look at me! Look me in the face!—Oh, if I could but understand what your eyes are saying! No, I cannot see your mind in them as once I could; those eyes, that were my very life, they are blinded to me!

[*She begins to weep.*]

ATAYDE:

Don't let yourself be seen like this!—It was rightly said that a soldier and a merchant should have no wife!

DOÑA LEONOR:

No wife . . . and no conscience!

[*They go out. It has been growing dark. Now* FATHER XAVIER *and* MATTHEW *enter, quickly, as if fleeing from something.* MATTHEW *carries a lamp.*]

XAVIER:

This way. . . .

MATTHEW:

Father Francis!

XAVIER:

We're here—say nothing.

MATTHEW:

Why do you fly like a thief, when you have done so much good?

XAVIER:

What good?

MATTHEW:

Father, I was close beside you, and I saw. The child was dead when you arrived. He was dead, and cold as ice.

XAVIER:

Don't be talking nonsense.

MATTHEW:

Father. . . .

XAVIER:

I say that he was sleeping.

[*By the left, an Indian has run in, like a wounded animal, terrified and sobbing.*]

MATTHEW:

Is not that somebody crying?

[*He raises the lamp and discovers the* NEGRO.]

XAVIER:

Who comes at this hour?

MATTHEW:

Who is that?

PATAMAR:

[*Bending, almost kneeling*] Don't—don't hurt me!

XAVIER:

Who is he?

MATTHEW:

A patamar—one who runs with messages—he has lost his way.

PATAMAR:

Stranger; do not hurt me, stranger!

XAVIER:

Do not fear; no one will hurt you.

PATAMAR:

I believe you. Your eyes are gentle, like a deer's.

XAVIER:

What has befallen you?

PATAMAR:

Oh, they will slay me with rods if I go back to the city. White man, save me! If you save me, I promise that I will find the mother-o'-pearl that is deepest in the ocean—for you.

XAVIER:

You need not promise it. I am not in that business. Who is your master?

PATAMAR:

Are you going to tell him of me, Stranger?

MATTHEW:

The white man wishes to save you. Speak openly to him; he is good.

PATAMAR:

White man, my master has not kindly eyes like yours; not a deer's eyes, but the eyes of a wolf, the eyes of a jackal. I have lost his message, and he will kill me if I return.

XAVIER:

What is his name?

PATAMAR:

Don Alvaro. . . .

XAVIER:

De Atayde?

PATAMAR:

Yes, yes; that's it. . . . But you will not tell him that I have lost his money?

XAVIER:

What money?

PATAMAR:

A few days ago, he bade me go to the Kingdom of Macassar, and he gave me a present to be carried to the Chief and the Brahman of that people—it was twenty pieces of gold. He knows that I am faithful; he could trust me. I never lost his messages; I never touched his gold.

XAVIER:

Tell me now how you lost the money.

PATAMAR:

The sun was burning me like fire. I wanted to bathe in the river. The wallet slipped open. The money fell in the water. It was like little fishes of gold, and the river carried it away.

[*Sobbing.*]

XAVIER:

Oh, do not cry.

PATAMAR:

Why do you care if I cry? . . . Stranger—stranger: will you give me twenty pieces of gold like those?

XAVIER:

You have brought your ship to a good port for such a cargo!

[*Showing his empty pockets.*]

MATTHEW:

The white man has not so much as a handful of fresh dates!

PATAMAR:

My master will kill me with rods.

XAVIER:

He shall not kill you.

PATAMAR:

I cannot go to Macassar. The letter says that I bear the money with me.

XAVIER:

What letter?

PATAMAR:

The letter that the white man gave me.

XAVIER:

Where is it?

PATAMAR:

I have it here; it stayed in the bottom of my wallet. I cannot deliver it without the money.

XAVIER:

[*Suddenly inspired*] Let me see that letter.

PATAMAR:

Stranger: it was for the great Brahman of Macassar; he can read.

XAVIER:

Negro, show me the letter.

PATAMAR:

Here it is.

XAVIER:

[*Giving it to* MATTHEW *and taking the torch*] I do not understand this matter, Matthew. Read it you.

MATTHEW:

[*Reading*] "*Lord: grace be with you and the peace of heaven. With the messenger who bears this, I send twenty pieces of money as a pledge and testimony of my respect and regard. . .*"

XAVIER:

[*Ironic*] I am glad to hear such cordial sentiments from Don Alvaro. What else?

MATTHEW:

"*The last sacks of cinnamon have come to port. Soon, with the passing of winter and the rains, the white missionary—of whom I told you—will set forth with the caravan that I am making ready. I deliver him into your hands. You know that he is not my friend, and I am your friend.*" [MATTHEW *repeats* "*I deliver him into your hands*", *as if he cannot believe his eyes.*] Father Francis!

XAVIER:

[*Calmly, raising the lamp higher*] Well? . . . Can't you see to read on, Matthew?

MATTHEW:

I see more than I would wish to see.

XAVIER:

Well then . . . go on reading.

MATTHEW:

"Remember our talk, when I was last in Macassar. I follow him, and will be there soon after him. By the time that I arrive, it must be done." Father Xavier!

XAVIER:

How gentle and loving must have been the Master's gaze when He turned His eyes on Judas, saying: "One of you shall betray Me!" Well now, I too wish this letter to reach its destination.

PATAMAR:

I cannot carry it unless I have the money.

MATTHEW:

But . . . Father! . . .

XAVIER:

Yes . . . Matthew: for months past, I have pleaded with Don Alvaro to arrange for me this journey to Macassar. . . . And this is the only reason for which he has fulfilled my wish. To hurt me he will do that which he would not do to please me.

MATTHEW:

But you go, Father, to be delivered over to devouring wolves.

XAVIER:

I go to throw my life and the Gospel into the balance. At last, O Lord, here is something that I can do to serve Thee! O little messenger, hurry you like the lark that flies over the meadow; you carry my dreams and the flower of my desires!

PATAMAR:

White man, I cannot go unless you give me the money.

MATTHEW:

This will save you!

XAVIER:

[*Raising eyes to heaven*] I do not ask to be saved thus. [*Transfigured, breathing hard*] Lord, Lord, do not disdain to hear my voice: grant that Thy servant may taste of the cup of Thine anguish in the garden! Thou didst turn a cheek, that Thou shouldst be betrayed by a kiss; oh, for this betrayal that is plotted, grant that I may have the price!

MATTHEW:

Father Xavier! . . .

XAVIER:

[*In his natural manner again; searching his pockets; addresses the* PATAMAR] Do you know?—perhaps, a cure can be found for your misfortune!

PATAMAR:

You will give me the money, white man?

XAVIER:

Perhaps . . . in this pocket. . . .

MATTHEW:

Father!

XAVIER:

Be silent, Matthew! [*He has taken some gold pieces from a pocket.*] Perhaps, there is enough here.

[*He gives them to the* PATAMAR, *who receives them, kneeling.*]

PATAMAR:

May the gods bless your hand!—Can this be true?—There are twenty pieces of gold, like those I lost, Stranger!

XAVIER:

You must not tell anybody of this.

MATTHEW:

Father, is this possible?

XAVIER:

Nor you either! . . . And now, away with you to Macassar and deliver the letter and the money. Tell them to get ready a sponge soaked in vinegar and gall; let them weave a crown of thorns . . . and fashion a cross of wood.

PATAMAR:

I—I do not understand.

XAVIER:

No matter. Hurry; and be silent, messenger.

PATAMAR:

[*Kissing the coins before he puts them in the wallet*] O white man, your pieces of money smell of flowers; flowers that I never knew.

XAVIER:

It is merely that I carry spices in my pockets.

PATAMAR:

Let me but kiss the hem of your garment.

XAVIER:

[*Withdrawing himself*] Go, negro; do not let them find you here.

PATAMAR:

I go.

[*He leaves, at the left.*]

MATTHEW:

I never can consent to this!

XAVIER:

Do not you do as Saint Peter did, who boasted, and then denied the Master before the cock had crowed three times. Be silent . . . and may God over-rule all!

MATTHEW:

But Atayde. . . .

XAVIER:

I am content . . . but that name comes upon me like a weight, when I hear it. . . . His soul, Matthew, his soul! When I try to grasp it, it slips from my hands, like water through a sieve! His soul!—Oh, what grief, grief!—His soul, his soul!

MATTHEW:

Can you find it in you to pity the hangman when he has his rope about your neck?

XAVIER:

'Tis God Who rules all. . . . That man is but the instrument of His will.

[*A tumult of voices has been heard, drawing near.*]

VOICES [*within*]:

A miracle! . . .

Where is the Father? . . .
This way. . . .

MATTHEW:

They come seeking you.

XAVIER:

Hide the light, Matthew!

VOICES [*nearer*]:

Answer, Father! . . .
Where is he? . . .
I saw him at this side. . . .

XAVIER:

Run! They are coming!

[*A number of women and men, negroes and Malays, with torches, enter; at their head,* THE MOTHER *who had called for* FATHER XAVIER.]

A MAN:

Here he is!

THE MOTHER:

[*Falling at the* FATHER'S *feet*] O, blessed, blessed!

A WOMAN:

Who is this who flies, as if afraid, like one who has done a crime—flies, when he has done so much good?

THE MOTHER:

[*Kissing his feet*] Father, Father!

XAVIER:

Do not weep!

THE MOTHER:

These tears are tears of love, and tears of joy. Let all

you hear what he has done for me!—he has awakened my flower that slept, he has brought back my darling!

XAVIER:

Hush!—do not listen to her. It is not certain.

THE MOTHER:

[*Witholding him, by the knees*] How not, if my child was dead, when he came? Ice-cold he was, and stiff; my hand felt him; he was cold as the snows on the mountains; there was no light in his eyes; he was yellow like the flower of rosemary. I, like a mad woman, cried: "Xavier, send me Father Xavier." "And what can the Father do?" they asked me. "No matter; a Mother asks it; when a Mother mourns a child, she asks for the impossible." And the Father came, and he touched him with his staff . . . and he lived again!

XAVIER:

He was but sleeping! Take no notice of this foolish good woman!

THE MOTHER:

It is true. . . . I swear to you all that the child came back to life when he but touched him lightly with his staff. . . .

XAVIER:

Anyway, it was God. . . . Between His goodness and your faith, I was no more than the go-between.

A MAN:

This is a Saint!

XAVIER:

Oh, silent, be silent, I beg you!

A WOMAN:

Throw flowers before him!

XAVIER:

[*Flying from them by main force*] I am but one sinner more among all sinners. You are foolish poor folk and dreamers ; I did no more than waken a sleeping child. No prodigy, no rare favour here!

[*He has freed himself, and is going out at the left, when he turns and raises his hands to Heaven, with a sudden transition.*]

But pray you to the Lord and praise Him, as if it had been so.

[CURTAIN]

ACT III

SCENE I

In Macassar: at the door of the dwelling of the Chief of the tribe, over which is a kind of bamboo awning. Desert background.

[TWO INDIANS *are before the* CHIEF'S *door, making a basket.*]

FIRST INDIAN:

Have you the basket of bread and herbs prepared for the sacrifice?

SECOND INDIAN:

All is measured and ready.

FIRST INDIAN:

Come, then.

SECOND INDIAN:

Wait!—Do you not see a cloud out yonder, where the sun covers the sand with sparkling crystal?

FIRST INDIAN:

I see it.

SECOND INDIAN:

It must be the Portuguese.

FIRST INDIAN:

Warn the Chief!

SECOND INDIAN:

[*At the door of the dwelling, with a bow.*] Lord, a caravan is approaching from afar off.

[THE CHIEF *comes forth, followed by an Indian who performs the part of a* CHAMBERLAIN; *behind is the* GRAND BRAHMAN.]

THE CHIEF:

It must be the Whites. Now that the skies are clear and the sands are fit to travel, it is their time to come. Do you not think so, Brahman?

BRAHMAN:

May Brahma send us prosperity, in their coming!

CHAMBERLAIN:

I see wagons and oxen.

THE CHIEF:

They seem to be halting. It grows dark. Light a torch and raise it, lest they lose their way in the sands.

FIRST INDIAN:

[*Ascending a palm, bearing a torch*] White man, ho! —White man, here, here!

CHAMBERLAIN:

They have sighted us.

THE CHIEF:

Wave the torch!

CHAMBERLAIN:

One is making for us.

THE CHIEF:

This White will be the man of whom the Portuguese

told us. Do you see him coming, Brahman? He travels barefoot, in a ragged habit.

FIRST INDIAN:

This way, this way!

THE CHIEF:

He is bending like a reed under the wind from the South.

CHAMBERLAIN:

The road to this place is rocky. . . . Come hither, White Man!

[FATHER XAVIER *enters, barefoot, ragged, leaning on a stick.* MATTHEW *follows him, with bags.*]

XAVIER:

May the peace of the Lord be upon you all!

[THE CHIEF *sits at his door, eyes* XAVIER *closely, then signs to him to approach. The* BRAHMAN *stands at some distance.*]

THE CHIEF:

Come!—You must have been travelling many days by the roads?

XAVIER:

More than ten.

THE CHIEF:

You must be footsore and wounded with much walking. Our law bids us wash the feet of the wayfarer.

MATTHEW:

[*Coming forward with childlike simplicity*] It is not needed. He has travelled afoot by the hard roads, but I know that every night, when he was sleeping, the jackals came and licked his hands and feet.

THE CHIEF:

The jackals?

XAVIER:

Hush!—this good fellow was so wearied out as we walked across the desert that he slept heavily and hardly knew when he was awake: he dreamed, and thinks that what he *dreamed*, he *saw*.

THE CHIEF:

And what are you seeking?

XAVIER:

To preach the Faith, to preach the Good and True.

THE CHIEF:

That is, to attack our own beliefs.

XAVIER:

Say rather that I ask leave to compare them. Suppose that one who had been blind should suddenly come to see, on a bright moonlit night; he would surely believe that in all the heavens there was no grander light than the moon. Then, as the dawn appeared, he would begin to doubt; and when at last he saw the risen sun he would know that it was the brighter by far.

THE CHIEF:

[*After pausing and reflecting*] And you come?

XAVIER:

I come from Spain, which is a rock at the end of the earth, in the far-off West, bathed by the ocean that we call the Shadowy Sea; it is God's granary; it has grain enough to cover the earth with corn. See you, at the winnowing of this grain of which I speak, I am a grain of wheat which the wind has carried by hazard hither.

THE CHIEF:

Do not think to overawe us with your words. Say plainly, why come you to this land?

XAVIER:

Half in the name of war and half in the name of love; I carry the truth in my hands; I come to preach Christ.

THE CHIEF:

Then you will be one of those, it seems, who are called Christians. . . . You know that in Ceylon your fellows were put to death with knives?

XAVIER:

What matter? Silver shines more brightly for hard scouring. To die for Christ is peace. Those martyrs of Ceylon will be the seed of Christ; and their graves, that are the open gorges in the rocks, will be for all ages open mouths to confess Christ—Christ always!

CHAMBERLAIN:

[*Shouting*] Remember that you are before the Chief! Have a care of this bold language! Do not dare too far!

XAVIER:

[*Looking about him in feigned surprise, till his eyes fall on the immobile* BRAHMAN] Who is it that is deaf? . . . The holy man?

CHAMBERLAIN:

Nobody is deaf.

XAVIER:

Then pardon!—but why shout at me? Are you trying to strengthen your own confidence with roaring?

THE CHIEF:

The White man is right. We must speak in turn. Let us begin by hearing what he has to say.

BRAHMAN:

[*Solemnly breaking silence*] Let not yourself be led astray by the talk of a madman!

XAVIER:

Well then, if it is so dangerous to listen to the mad missionary, it will be well to hear first what the Wise Man says. Expound to the poor stranger the lofty science of the Brahmans!

BRAHMAN:

My science is occult; it is secret.

XAVIER:

[*Emboldened by the* CHIEF'S *silence, goes to the attack*] That's enough! You Brahmans, what are you but a caste of idlers and mystery-makers? For whom do you guard your wonderful secrets?

BRAHMAN:

[*Snuffling, to conceal his confusion*] In all things there are grades of initiation. . . .

XAVIER:

Why all this hugger-mugger? The true Faith, Brahman, is not a light for some few initiates alone. . . . The Lord whom I adore, He Whom I preach, He lit with the light of dawn the fields of Galilee; that which He came to teach us, we wish not to make into a secret doctrine. No, O secretive man, it is otherwise with us. Christ taught upon the mountain, and on the lake and on the sea!

THE CHIEF:

[*To* BRAHMAN] What answer have you to that?

BRAHMAN:

I tell him that it is not given to all mortals to arrive at the celestial secrets of the truth.

XAVIER:

So, not all men are equal?

BRAHMAN:

Blaspheme not. I—I came came forth from the head of Brahma.

XAVIER:

Friend, you are but dust that a word of God has ennobled.

BRAHMAN:

Speak courteously!—your words are unfitting. Before God and your catechism, all may bc equal, but I say to you that a pariah and an outcast never will be the same as a Brahman, like me.

XAVIER:

By what law is this so?

BRAHMAN:

Because the great Brahma, when he makes all men, gives them different natures. The pariah is born of his foot, and the Brahman of his head; and thus, even at birth, the different natures of our different castes are stamped upon us. . . .

XAVIER:

As for my God—He would gather all men into His heart! That is my teaching.

THE CHIEF:

There is much beauty in it.

XAVIER:

The Truth is always beautiful.

BRAHMAN:

And so is fantasy!

THE CHIEF:

But tell me: if we had not these Brahmans whom you call mystery-makers, who would offer for us the gifts which the gods consume?

XAVIER:

Ho!—so your gods eat? You are sure that it is not your Brahmans?

BRAHMAN:

[*Choleric with indignation*] You insult me!

THE CHIEF:

Control your indignation and shew us reason against his arguments.

XAVIER:

Aye, tell me the commandments of your law.

BRAHMAN:

White man, my commandments are not mysterious.

XAVIER:

And what does your god command?

BRAHMAN:

To drink naught but water, and not to eat the forbidden animals.

XAVIER:

A poor, weak rule of life! For in truth God cares for

that which proceeds from the mouth, not that which goes into it. Your doctrine has but little thought for the interior man, the soul. Do not use your mouth to utter lies, I say, do not befoul it with anger—and then eat what you like! You build all on outside appearances; but the eyes of the Lord see through to the evil within. Let the sinner persevere in sin, and you will tell him that all will be made right with the eternal justice if he puts cow's dung on his head! . . . My faith is deeper. It begins, not where appearances begin but where they end. You must go down into the depths to find it, as the pearl is found in the deeps of the sea.

THE CHIEF:

What is this Faith of yours?

BRAHMAN:

Forbid him to proceed!

THE CHIEF:

Why so, Brahman?

BRAHMAN:

Because so you will serve the gods well.

THE CHIEF:

And maybe serve you even better?

XAVIER:

You spend your evenings and the hours of dawn prostrate before Father Sun; for none has told you of the One God Who created that sun which you adore. Of this God, to Whom no other god is equal, I come to tell you; and in His Name, to teach you how He came to earth for love of mortal men, and lay in a manger, clothed in human flesh, and taking JESUS as His Name . . .

BRAHMAN:

This Christian lies! [*He spits in* XAVIER'*s face.*]

THE CHIEF:

[*Rising wrathfully*] Brahman!

[*Frightened, the* BRAHMAN *retires some steps. The* CHIEF *stands amazed as* XAVIER *quietly wipes his face and proceeds.*]

XAVIER:

As we were saying . . . Christ God made Himself man in order to teach us this celestial science which so many wise men have failed to learn: to forgive injuries and to return good for evil.

THE CHIEF:

What man is this, who answers insults in this fashion?

XAVIER:

To suffer for Christ is an honour. He gives me the courage. . . . I am a pitiful poor servant of so great a Lord.

THE CHIEF:

White man, your strange power overcomes me; you conquer me. Do a miracle now in my sight, and I promise to believe.

XAVIER:

Without miracles and signs it must be done. The true believer does not ask for proofs of the light; its brilliance is enough. . . . I am something more than a petty serpent-charmer! Without more light than faith you must plumb the very abyss; you must believe for the very scandal of the Cross! I speak in the Name of JESUS, Who was spat upon and scourged; His divine Flesh was torn, and He died nailed upon a Cross.

THE CHIEF:

Then . . . you come to us with the doctrine of One Who was condemned . . . ?

XAVIER:

Of One Who was condemned for love; for He loved us in such a manner that He gave us life by His death, and hope through His sorrow. I speak of a generous Lord Who had a word like honey for all; He was mindful of pariahs, and He bade little children come near to Him. I speak of a God Whose Hands were nailed wide upon the Cross, and Whose Arms are opened with love for all sinners!

THE CHIEF:

White man, we would hear you tell us all that you believe.

XAVIER:

I do but ask your leave to be free to teach.

[DON ALVARO DE ATAYDE, *in high travelling boots, has entered at the right.*]

ATAYDE:

What is this? Are they listening to your sermons in Macassar, too?

XAVIER:

Here comes the faithful friend, overflowing with kind intentions. . . . [*Pointing to the* INDIANS] . . . The lions in Daniel's den are tame already! . . .

ATAYDE:

You have no thanks for me, despite all that I have done to bring you here.

XAVIER:

Aye, sure of my destruction!

ATAYDE:

[*Almost throwing himself on* XAVIER] No!!

THE CHIEF:

[*Rising, and commanding* ATAYDE *with a gesture*] Cease! This man is my guest; his person is sacred.

XAVIER:

Yes, cease, Atayde. It does not stand to reason (as you see) that the Lord should send me all the way to the East . . . just that I should die at the hands of a Portuguese.

ATAYDE:

What are you saying, Xavier?

XAVIER:

You thought that you had exposed me to the last rigours, here in Macassar; but they have proved softer than you expected.

THE CHIEF:

The white man is right. I suspect, Portuguese, that you planned his destruction here in your own interests. . . . But let the Christian have no fear. He has not spoken in vain. Let him live here as long as he wishes . . . for a true Indian would not have the blood of the just on his hands. . . . Portuguese, if you want your money . . .

ATAYDE:

[*Pretending not to understood*] What money?

THE CHIEF:

I say, again, Stranger, if you want . . .

ATAYDE:

I want nothing!

XAVIER:

You need not be scandalized; I know all about it. I saw the twenty pieces of gold that were the price of a sin. . . . Was it not a high value that you set on me? They gave thirty pieces of silver for Christ!

ATAYDE:

I say that it is a lie, Xavier—this that you have said.

XAVIER:

Did these eyes lie, which saw a certain letter?

ATAYDE:

[*Beside himself as if to spring on* XAVIER] I will have to do myself what these fools failed to do!

THE CHIEF:

Do you dare to attempt this crime, before us? . . . Seize him!

[*The* INDIANS *leap at* ATAYDE, *but* XAVIER *interposes his own body.*]

XAVIER:

Hush!—now will I defend him! [*They reel back, astonished.*]

THE CHIEF:

What! He planned to murder you. Do you raise your hand in his defence?

XAVIER:

He is my brother, as well as my enemy. Let nobody injure him, I say!

THE CHIEF:

Are you a madman?

XAVIER:

I am a Christian. . . . Vengeance has no part in what I teach; my faith forbids revenge. . . . Atayde, henceforth I will be the guard posted to protect your sinful life. You shall not die now; I know you are in sin. Let no one dare to touch a hair of your head! [*To the* INDIANS] . . . . And now behold me kiss the hand that sought to slay me. This is the new lesson, that I have come to teach you!

ATAYDE:

[*His head sinking*] Always, you end by winning.

XAVIER:

This is because God fights on Xavier's side. . . . Atayde, do not pit yourself yourself against the two!

THE CHIEF:

So be it. Atayde shall be protected, as you ask it. . . . And now, White man, the moment that you wished has come; we will hear your teaching.

XAVIER:

Matthew, if the Chief allows it, summon the people to my presence.

THE CHIEF:

Whosoever desires, let him come!

MATTHEW:

[*Having taken the little bell from his bags, shakes it*

towards the plain] Come all ye who wish to hear the White man; he tells the new doctrine of Life and of Salvation. . . . This is excellent knowledge; to know these things is very good! . . .

[MEN, WOMEN *and* CHILDREN *enter.*]

XAVIER:

Let all the people be seated before me. . . . And let none fear; I come not in the name of war or any hurt, my words contain nothing but the good. [*When they are seated, before him, he raises his hands and begins to preach*] . . . . I come to speak to you of One Only God, Creator of heaven and earth . . .

[CURTAIN]

ACT III

SCENE II [1]

The Quay at Malacca. At the right the figure-head of a galley which is moored to the quay, a sail drooping; mariners go up and down, carrying loads aboard the vessel. DON DUARTE DE GAMA, *Portuguese sea-captain, talks with* MATTHEW.

MATTHEW:

Is it true, Don Duarte, that your ships will sail to-day for Japan?

DON DUARTE:

I cannot delay longer. The typhoon season draws on; the seas will be over-perilous soon for navigation.

MATTHEW:

[*With signs of fear*] And it is true that Father Francis is going with you?

DON DUARTE:

[*Smiling*] Perhaps.

MATTHEW:

[*Almost weeping*] Oh, oh, tell me for sure! Is he going from Malacca?

DON DUARTE:

Perhaps. . . . I cannot tell you any more. . . .

1 Owing to difficulty of presentation, this scene was not acted in the original performance.

MATTHEW:

But, please . . .

DON DUARTE:

Here he comes, who will be able to answer you.

[*By the left enter* XAVIER, *with* MANSILLA, FATHER COSME, *the Portuguese* JUAN FERNÁNDEZ, *and* YAGIRO, *a Japanese.*]

MATTHEW:

O, Father Xavier, dear Father Xavier; do not deny me the truth!

XAVIER:

[*Soothing* MATTHEW] The wind tells all things! I wished to spare you these painful moments, Matthew; but it is easier to hide light with a riddle than to keep a secret in a city.

MATTHEW:

And what will become of us in Malacca, if you go?

XAVIER:

It is time for the young broods to be able to fly alone.

DON DUARTE:

Do the Indies love you so poorly, Father, that you must fly from them to some other land?

XAVIER:

It is almost so. To be a missionary in the Indies is to be only half a missionary. To-day, this place is as much Europe as India; you have to wrestle with Christians as well as natives—one and the other at the same time. I am dreaming of some distant world where the wrestling is between the unbelievers on one side, and on the other, Christ—and none to come between.

MANSILLA:

Do not let your Reverence be displeased; you leave behind you a goodly harvest gathered.

XAVIER:

Ah, much kissing of my hand, much coming to hear me preach; but they have not closed the slave market nor ceased to trade in negroes.

DON DUARTE:

Then, the passengers for the ship are . . . ?

XAVIER:

These go with me: Father Cosme de Torres, my brother priest, and Juan Fernández, my friend, whose humility has forbidden him to be my novice . . . and Yagiro, this good Japanese, whom God sent across my path like a lucky star.

MANSILLA:

It was through him—was it not, Father?—that you came to think of this new enterprise of Japan?

XAVIER:

My great impatience was growing daunted; I had found no fire to match the fire of my desire; and then I chanced to fall into talk with Yagiro. It was of God we spoke. I told him, as far as I could, the truth concerning Christ and His teaching; and then Yagiro began to question me. . . . O, brothers, do you know how a master is cheered when a pupil besieges him for knowledge? It is like light in darkness, or an answering voice in the desert. . . . Yagiro told me that his people, the people of Japan, are lovers and seekers of truth, and my soul was afire within me as he spoke. I was like the pilot who cries out "Land, land!" as he sights it over the waters; I wanted to go through the city, shouting: "At last, at last, I have found the desire to know, I have found souls that are seeking God!" Forthwith, in my heart, I resolved to travel thither, to that people which has asked and hungered for the truth, through many centuries: I go, to bring them the answer!

[*Hurriedly enter from the left men and women, among them* DOÑA LEONOR, ATAYDE, *and the* VICAR-GENERAL of Malacca.]

DOÑA LEONOR:

[*Tearfully*] Is it true, is it true, that your Reverence is sailing for Japan?

ATAYDE:

Are you not afraid of the sea?

XAVIER:

Atayde, I am sorry that I am leaving you—alone with your conscience.

DON DUARTE:

We hoist anchor to-day.

VICAR-GENERAL:

Look you, Father, nobody dares to set foot on land among that dangerous people.

XAVIER:

That's why we do not get to Heaven; we do not meet the folk who would send us there.

VICAR-GENERAL:

But those dour people, their souls are like ice; they never were taught better.

XAVIER:

Why, see, if you wished to persuade me not to undertake this journey, you went the worst way about it; no, but you did your best to enflame my fervour afresh . . if you fear a bad harvest, should the sower never sow?

DON DUARTE:

Father, it is time.

MATTHEW:

[*Sobbing*] It is cruel to be separated from you.

XAVIER:

[*Concealing emotion*] My friends . . .

DOÑA LEONOR:

You are leaving India widowed.

XAVIER:

[*Embracing* MANSILLA] May God pour His favours on you, Brother. . . . Do not forget me and my dreams and all my happiness here. . . . Watch over and water that which I sowed; for the young crop still is green. . . . Comorene, that I watched over; and Ceylon, my pain and my reward; those isles of Moluccas that are the roses of my heart and the consolation of my sorrows! Watch carefully over them, I say, as if you were watching over my rest and protecting my happiness. . . . These are pieces of my life, that I am leaving behind me here. . . .

And you, Father Vicar, go on with my work. You have seen what is needed. Preach to the people every day; and when you speak of Christ, Father, do not speak with such abandon as may frighten the spirits of some or discourage the novices. Speak less of His just anger than of His grace and His forgiveness. Be not satisfied with sermons within the church, behind closed doors. Go out and talk in the market places and the harvest fields; fear nobody and nothing! Christ, remember, lived in a stable, and I, for Him, eat, drink and gossip, aye, and even play chess . . . in hope that, as I play, I may win a soul from the devil. For Christ, in all things there are opportunities. If I thought on any day that I could save some soul at the dance, I swear to you that I'd go dancing! . . .

Señora Doña Leonor . . .

My faithful Matthew . . .

[DOÑA LEONOR *kisses his soutane, weeping. He lays his hands on* MATTHEW'*s head.*]

MATTHEW:

My soul is parting from my body!

ATAYDE:

[*Whom* XAVIER *salutes coldly*] I am sorry that you must go.

XAVIER:

[*Taking a little crucifix from his neck and giving it*] And you, please, take this cross that I would give you. God sent you in my path for my instruction and for my good. . . . Should I not feel, here too, the bitterness of parting? [*Leading towards the ship*] Adieu to you all!

MATTHEW:

Oh, who dares to let the Father go on such a journey?

MANSILLA:

Yes, yes; we cannot let it be! [*They surround him and hold him.*]

XAVIER:

I'll never get away if you hold me so tenderly. . . . Let me go! If you stand in my way, I will throw myself into the sea, here and now; for I will get there, if I have to walk the waves.

[*He breaks free, and goes up into the ship, followed by* FATHER COSME, YAGIRO, JUAN FERNÁNDEZ *and* DON DUARTE.]

MATTHEW:

Father! . . . Father!

XAVIER:

[*Going aboard, without turning his gaze*] Enough of all this, child! Listen: I leave you all my love, and no more talk about it!

DON DUARTE:

Hoist the anchor! . . . Let go the cable! . . .

[*Chains sound*]

MATTHEW:

Father! . . .

DOÑA LEONOR:

[*Sobbing*] Oh, oh!

XAVIER:

[*Hands crossed on bosom, at foot of the great sail, watches the sea, shoulders turned to the quay*] Lord: the infinity of the ocean fills my soul. . . . At last, at last, Xavier goes to undertake a work that is worthy of the toil!

DON DUARTE:

Haul in the sheets! [*The sail beats as in a great wind*] An excellent wind! I never thought that we'd get such a breeze in this season.

XAVIER:

It is the wind of my fortune, straining for ever towards the East.

[CURTAIN]

ACT III

SCENE III

In Funay, Japan. Interior of a bamboo hut, with some scant furniture; door at the left. YAGIRO, FATHER COSME *and* JUAN FERNÁNDEZ, *sleeping on the ground.* FATHER XAVIER *in the centre, in ecstatic vigil; moonlight filters through the walls to his face.*

XAVIER:

Thou dost deny me consolation, in relieving me of yearning, of yearning as for death! . . . Oh, if Thou makest Heaven of this life, shall I not become attached to life and fear to lose it? [*Pause ; a strange smile, as for some interior consolation*] Enough of these celestial lights, whereby Thou piercest to the deepest shadows of my being! Lord, Lord—give me a little share of thorns; enough now of roses for to-day! [*Without, a loud guttural shout, like a signal.* YAGIRO *rises and looks through the gaps in the door*] That shout?

YAGIRO:

It comes from the warrior-folk, it is the sign of the Bonzos. They must be very near.

XAVIER:

Are we surrounded?

YAGIRO:

Yes, Father. We are taken on all sides. . . . If Don

Duarte who brought us to Japan knew the plight that you are in, he would come to rescue you.

XAVIER:

I do not know where he has gone with his expedition. . . . Is it snowing?

YAGIRO:

[*Looking out by the door*] It stopped for a while, and then began again. The whole meadow is white. Every watch-fire looks like a flower of flame.

XAVIER:

If God does not appease the madness of these unbelievers, those flowers will fashion for us the crown of martyrdom.

YAGIRO:

Oh, Father, how it grieves me that I urged you to come to this country! I told you of my people, that you could trust them, and I deceived myself.

XAVIER:

You were not deceived. Throughout Japan, Yagiro, I found souls that were thirsting to receive the Faith. These Bonzos—they are to Japan what the Brahmans are, yonder, to India—they pursue me and would slay me because they see that my triumph would turn the people against them, and would overthrow their power. They are striving to save the privilege of their caste. Not for the love of truth they fight, but for secret interests. . . . Always, mark you, the thirty pieces of silver for some Judas, to betray the Lord!

[*Shouts again,* FATHER COSME *and* JUAN FERNÁNDEZ *rise and peer forth.*]

FATHER COSME:

The Bonzos!

JUAN FERNÁNDEZ:

[*Unable to restrain a sign of terror*] O God!

XAVIER:

Sons, eyes front, to face death! Did we not come here to sow the seed? We have laboured, and now we must water the seed that we have sown!

YACIRO:

The Bonzos know that the King of Japan has treated us well for the sake of the goodwill of Portugal. Now in the night, when there is no help near, they attack us, in secret.

[*A noise at the right, as if the bamboos were parted.*]

XAVIER:

Do you hear that?

A VOICE [*without*]:

Father!

XAVIER:

Who is that?

THE VOICE:

Friends, friends, Father Xavier!

XAVIER:

Speak your name!

[*Rods are broken down*; DON DUARTE *appears.*]

—Who? . . . Don Duarte!

DON DUARTE:

Brothers, do you not know your peril? Yonder, in the rear, there are a hundred men.

XAVIER:

[*Calmly*] —And still more in front.

DON DUARTE:

—And you say it, with that peaceful look? Listen: I have my boat and my people, very near. I saw the signals of fire and I guessed your danger. I crept here by the paths through the rushes without being seen. . . . Come now, all is ready for you to escape. If they did not see me, they will not see you.

[*All move, as if to go, except* XAVIER, *who restrains them.*]

XAVIER:

That is what Christ's disciples did, on the night when He was taken. . . . I will not deny the Lord in the court of Caiphas. I will not be that workman who deserts his crop when the field has come into flower.

DON DUARTE:

There are fires on all sides! . . . Father, if these savage people take you, they will crucify you.

XAVIER:

Could it be? But that's too good to come to pass.

DON DUARTE:

What are you saying?

XAVIER:

Oh, to perish for His love!—and on a cross! . . . Friends, already the dawn is reddening in the sky.

DON DUARTE:

There is no time to lose!

XAVIER:

Who speaks of loss, when the bud at last is breaking into flower? To lose? What if we are about to win all—all—all?

FATHER COSME:

[*Kneeling before the Father*] In death or life, let me be at your side! Oh, in the fiery harvest that your zeal desires, may I be gathered from the soil like a fallen ear of corn!

JUAN FERNÁNDEZ:

And I, and I!

YAGIRO:

Your faith gives courage to us all.

XAVIER:

[*To* DON DUARTE] Steal you away without being seen. . . .

DON DUARTE:

I will not leave you. . . . When these folk seize the house, let them find one sinner in the reckoning! My people are very near. I will go out and tell them to make away; for, in life or death, I'll stay and share the Father's fate.

XAVIER:

My son!

[DON DUARTE *goes out creeping.*]

YAGIRO:

It is dawning now, and I see them gathering. . . . They are coming, they are coming!

XAVIER:

Come, my sons, before me. . . . [*They gather round,*

some, kneeling; he addresses FATHER COSME.] Father, if I die, take you the command . . . and when I am dead, if any of you still lives, write for me to Father Ignatius over there in Rome, and tell him: that I died, thinking of him, and full of love. . . . I, whom he knew, that impatient one of Paris.

YAGIRO:

[*From the door*] Father, at this side I see branches flaming. They are going to burn us alive!

XAVIER:

Oh now, at last, Xavier is going to suffer something for Christ! . . . If I live, these lands will be won for God. If I die, I hope for glory. . . . My friends, on all hands, victory is about me! . . .

[*The bamboos move again, and* DON DUARTE *reappears, followed by men bearing weapons.*]

DON DUARTE:

Father!

XAVIER:

My son, what a host!

DON DUARTE:

Not one of them would go away. . . . I reached my men; I told them how it stands with you . . . And they said: "We'll all go, and die with you!"

A MAN:

Yes, yes, and with you and the Father!

ANOTHER:

Aye, all of us together!

DON DUARTE:

So if Heaven opens to you to-day, you'll carry a sheaf with you that is worthy of you.

[*Shouts; flames blaze beyond the bamboos.*]

YAGIRO:

Fire!

JUAN FERNÁNDEZ:

They are firing the house at all sides!

DON DUARTE:

We are not yet disarmed! Open these walls now, little by little. . . . .

[YAGIRO *and* FERNÁNDEZ *tear away planks of the door and the dawn on the snow is seen ;* JAPANESE *with lances and torches are surrounding the house ; they growl at the sight of the Portuguese with the Missionaries.*

DON DUARTE *advances to the threshold, with drawn sword.*]

. . . . Did you think that some poor missionaries were deserted here, in these walls, for you to roast? They have companions, look you, and so much the worse for you! . . . [*Raising the sword*] . . . We'll see now if you are as brave in making war on Christ when beside His Cross there is the sword of Portugal!

[*The* JAPANESE *raise hands and shout insistently.* DON DUARTE *questions* YAGIRO]

What are they saying? Interpret!

YAGIRO:

They demand a parley.

DON DUARTE:

Then tell them to send forward one man.

[YAGIRO *goes through the door; a* JAPANESE *approaches him with polite signs and they speak.*]

What is he saying?

YAGIRO:

He says that no one intends harm to the Portuguese or to insult their arms. . . .

DON DUARTE:

Tell them to have done with these Japanese civilities; I don't understand them, nor wish to understand them. Tell them that Father Xavier and all these Christians are our friends . . . and that all their city, old men and children, will answer for his life at my hands!

[YAGIRO *returns and speaks with the* JAPANESE, *who bows and nods, and lays down his arms.*]

YAGIRO:

He asks you to step on his sword and his dagger. . . . He says, that the King values highly the friendship of Portugal.

XAVIER:

[*Approaching*] These weapons have struck me a deeper, and a mortal wound! . . . These same folk who mocked our Christian gospel now grovel before us lest they should lose their trade in silks and bits of porcelain! . . . [*Coming before the Christians and addressing them in command*] But so it shall not be! Your weapons, come! Sheathe them! To me! [*Swords are sheathed, guns are lowered*] . . . . Father Xavier did not come to Japan to win his way with guns and swords. . . . Let none of you follow me! [*He draws the crucifix from his bosom, raises it in one hand, and turns to go forth*] . . . . And now behold me going forth, with no arms save my God, my faith, my cross—and this poor voice which they do not wish to hear! . . . Let none stir! [*He goes through the* JAPANESE*; they are paralysed with amazement and open to let him pass; some bow before him. To* DON DUARTE, *turning*] . . . . And you, when you go back to the West, tell how you have seen in the clear, bright light of the East, a people made to bow the head with no more weapons than the Cross! [*He continues to advance.*]

[CURTAIN]

EPILOGUE

Within the Castle of Xavier, in Navarre. A postern door at right, door towards inner chambers at left; a country fireplace, beside which are seated on easy chairs and stools, DON MIGUEL DE JASO *(*XAVIER'S *elder brother), another brother, and a sister (who is working at a spinning wheel) ;* DON MIGUEL *holds a letter.*

DON MIGUEL:

[*Reading*] . . . . "*And now, brothers, if the Lord wills, I am about to set out from Japan to China, where I hope to gather much grain for Christ. Thanks be to Heaven, we suffered among the Japanese some little, to make amends for the untold sins wherewith we have aggrieved the Precious Blood of Christ. The Lord preserved our life—a sure sign, since He grants us longer to live, that what we have done hitherto is but little. More work must be done, since God has given us more thread with which to do it.*

"*My health is somewhat frail, and my complexion has turned yellow ; for a year past my hair has been white. Yet I notice more and more that as the body grows fragile, the spirit grows all the more restless ; it carries me on my journeys like a wisp of straw on the wind.*

"*Do not forget me in your prayers ; in mine, I remember you all. An unprofitable servant of God and your brother, Francis.*"

BROTHER:

His impatience is with him still, as ever!

SISTER:

Always the same! he talks of journeying to China as he would talk here, when he was a child, of going off to the yard, or the garden, or the fishpond.

[*Knocks at the door.*]

A VOICE [*without*]:

Open, good folk, open to the poor!

SISTER:

Someone is calling?

MIGUEL:

Open the postern.

[*The door is opened. wind is heard without ; a beggar is seen.*]

BEGGAR:

Good folk, for charity, tell me if this is the castle of Xavier.

SISTER:

It is, good man.

BEGGAR:

Will you give a poor old man a little bread?

SISTER:

Wait while I go for it, and close the postern door ; for the south wind to day cuts like a knife.

[*She goes out by the left.*]

MIGUEL:

He wears a brown habit like the habit of St. Francis. . . .

[SISTER *returns with bread.*]

SISTER:

Take this, my friend. God protect you on your way!

BEGGAR:

And may He bless your household, if you have any in danger on land or sea!

SISTER:

[*Closing the door*] Holy Mother!

MIGUEL:

What's wrong?

SISTER.

A cold shiver came all over me.

MIGUEL:

[*Looking to the left*] Sister, has not the lamp before the Crucifix in the chapel gone out?

SISTER:

A blast of wind, perhaps . . .

MIGUEL:

You had better renew the oil and light it again.

[*The* SISTER *goes to the left; a pause. She is heard to cry out.*]

SISTER:

My God, my God!

MIGUEL:

What has happened?

BROTHER:

What is happening, sister?

SISTER:

[*Entering from the left, trembling*] I have seen it! I have seen it with these eyes! . . . I carried the taper to the little lamp. . . . I looked at the holy figure on the Crucifix above the altar. . . . There was a strange colour on the figure of Christ! . . . I touched it, and—look at my hands! They are wet with something red! I tell you that the figure was bleeding, bleeding. I saw it. Feel! [*The brothers touch her hand.*]

MIGUEL:

It is blood indeed.

BROTHER:

Warm blood!

SISTER:

O God!—something is happening to Francis in that far-off land!

[DON MIGUEL *takes the lamp which lights the scene; they all pass into the chapel, and the scene darkens.*]

SISTER'S VOICE:

Touch it!

MIGUEL:

Blood, yes, blood!

SISTER:

[*Sobbing*] Something is happening to Francis! Something is happening to Francis!

[*Light breaks the scene at the rear; the coast of the island of Sancian in Canton is seen, sand, sea and sky.* FATHER XAVIER *is seen entering. as he is de-*

scribed in the letter; he leans heavily on the shoulder of PAUL OF THE HOLY FAITH—*who is* YAGIRO, *now baptized.*]

XAVIER:

Ah, Brother Paul, Brother Paul, my body now is beginning to refuse to obey the soul. . . .

PAUL (YAGIRO):

Father!

XAVIER:

I see that this sea-shore of Sancian will be the last end of my path. [*Gazing over the sea; with extended arms; breathing heavily.*] To die, beholding the coasts of China, which was my goal, without reaching thither . . . like Moses, who died in the desert, with the Promised Land that was all his desire, so near beneath his eyes, but from his hands, so far!

PAUL (YAGIRO):

Do not say these things, Father!

XAVIER:

Paul, leave me a little while! [PAUL *retires to a corner, and looks on, weeping quietly.* XAVIER *falls on his knees.*] I am here, O God of all Graces, prostrate at Thy blessed feet, between these two vast solitudes of sea and the infinite sky. Aye now, with sails trailing in the water, with broken gear and useless helm, worn out by so much doing, Xavier's little boat comes to the end of its voyage. . . . [*Face illuminated by secret consolation.*] I have confessed Thee, Lord, unto the end, firmly and without shame; never have I hidden the light beneath a bushel. Hardship and sufferings have beset me; yet, O Lord, I overcame my weakness with Thy strength. Five talents Thou didst give to me, and I return unto Thee five more. . . .

Now as my light is flickering out I pray: bless Thou Ignatius Loyola . . . and care Thou for my people, the people of Spain . . . yea, Lord, and if the day ever should come when they forget Thee, and if their own works should fail to appease Thee and Thy justice, cast then also into the balance all that has been suffered for Thee—by Xavier.

[*He falls.* PAUL *approaches.*]

PAUL:

Father!

[*He tries to lift him.* XAVIER, *as if not noticing, speaks on.*]

XAVIER:

To die, to die, when so much remains to be done in Thy service.

[*He gropes.*]

PAUL:

What do you wish, Father?

XAVIER:

Don Alvaro de Atayde, who persecuted me. . . . Pray to Heaven to pardon him . . . for I die with that last prayer. . . . You will?

PAUL:

I will, Father.

XAVIER:

My eyes grow dark . . . and all my body is a living flame. . . .

[*He sinks to earth.*]

PAUL:

Father!

XAVIER:

[*Fighting still to hold his face towards heaven*] Lord, I trust in Thee. . . . [*A smile of joy*] Yes. . . . Thou dost not hide Thy face from me. . . . Thy servant . . . goes now . . . to seek Thee. . . . [*The head sinks down as he says:*]

In te, Domine, speravi.
Non confundar in æternum!

[*He collapses.* PAUL *still holds him, weeping.*]

[CURTAIN]